EQUALLY WED

EQUALLY WED

THE ULTIMATE GUIDE
to Planning Your LGBTQ+ Wedding

KIRSTEN PALLADINO

SEAL

ISBN 978-1-58005-670-0
ISBN 978-1-58005-671-7 (e-book)

Library of Congress Cataloging-in-Publication Data is available.

Published by
Seal Press
An imprint of Perseus Books, LLC
A subsidiary of Hachette Book Group, Inc.
1700 Fourth Street
Berkeley, California
Sealpress.com

Cover Design by Faceout Studio
Cover photo: Ruth Black
Interior Design by www.DominiDragoone.com
Illustrations © Kelly Angelovic

Printed in the United States of America
Distributed by Publishers Group West

TO MARIA,

my heart,

my joy,

my cheerleader,

my comfort,

my rock,

my forever

CONTENTS

Part Three
ESSENTIAL DETAILS

EQUALLY WED

FOREWORD

BY LANCE BASS AND MICHAEL TURCHIN

In the summer of 2015, the United States made a monumental leap forward when the Supreme Court finally ruled in favor of marriage equality for the LGBTQ+ community. What was once a distant hope for millions of gay and lesbian couples was now a fully realized right for all. For the first time, all LGBTQ+ couples could begin the exciting yet daunting task of planning legally recognized weddings, and as we began to plan our very own wedding, we were faced with a whole new set of questions and challenges.

When we immersed ourselves in the planning process, it quickly became apparent that there was a significant lack of resources available to us as a gay couple. We sought advice from our straight friends and families who had gone through the process themselves, but we soon realized that so many of the established traditions presented to us simply didn't make sense in our situation.

Do we get the same rings? What do we wear? Do we have a traditional ceremony? Where should we register? Which traditions should we keep and which should we create for ourselves? The list of questions we had seemed endless, and it only added unnecessary stress to what should have been one of the happiest days of our life together. As a result, we had to change our mind-sets, stop trying to fit our situation into the cookie-cutter notion of "traditional" marriage, and ultimately establish our own *new* traditions as a modern gay couple.

In an instant, frustration quickly transformed into excitement, and from that moment our creativity began to run wild! Instead of traditional young flower girls, we made a splash by using three of our gorgeous girlfriends who just happened to be supermodels. With no bride in the equation, why not?! Furthermore, we had a friend design three jaw-dropping gowns for our flower girls, reminiscent of couture wedding dresses. The end result was nothing short of amazing, and our guests are still talking about it to this day.

On another note, we made a point to use vendors and brands that had a record of supporting LGBTQ+ equality. From our flowers and food to our venue and tuxedos, we chose vendors who were truly excited to be a part of our union because without them and our other allies, it's a real possibility that we wouldn't be husbands today.

Ultimately our ideas expanded our imaginations even further. We encouraged our guests to dress as lavishly as possible—without fear of overshadowing us! In our minds, this day was just as much for our close friends and family as it was for us. We wanted our guests to feel the most beautiful they'd ever felt, and if that meant showing up in a wedding dress and veil, then by all means we welcomed it.

Looking back, we often wonder how we managed to pull off such an incredible evening with the lack of resources we found pertaining to same-sex weddings. Everything came together beautifully in the end, but if more information had been readily available to help us in regards to the unique planning and execution of our special day, we could have spared ourselves hours if not days worth of stress and worry. That is why *Equally Wed* is such a game changer in the world of same-sex weddings.

Equally Wed covers everything an engaged couple planning their wedding should consider from "I will" to "I do" with a modern approach tailored specifically to the needs of the LGBTQ+ community. From traveling to safe countries on the honeymoon to dealing with homophobic relatives when making the guest list to breaking out of society's so-called norms, *Equally Wed* leaves no stone unturned when it comes to successfully planning and executing that truly special day.

Lastly, we would be remiss if we didn't acknowledge the amazing woman who worked tirelessly making *Equally Wed* into a reality. Kirsten Palladino is an award-winning writer and editor, and one of the world's most notable experts on LGBTQ+ weddings. We first learned of Kirsten back in 2012, when she established National Marriage Equality Day in response to Mike Huckabee's National Chick-Fil-A Day, which applauded the restaurant chain's homophobic policies and funding of gay conversion therapy. Our paths then crossed again in 2014 when we hosted the "Toast to Marriage," an attempt to break the world record for the largest arms-linked toast (in support of marriage equality). We wholly respect the way that she believes in visibility, acceptance, and equality as we do, but also how she is relentless in fighting for it. Ultimately Kirsten isn't afraid to stand strong and use her voice, and now with *Equally Wed*, her voice and unique expertise are readily available to ensure that every LGBTQ+ person has the resources to plan the wedding of their dreams.

INTRODUCTION

I always wanted to get married. As a little girl, I dreamed of marriage, of being swept off my feet and finding that one person, my soul mate. I was often lost in some book, whether it was a sweet romance or some daring detective novel, romanticizing much of my future, including meeting my mate. By the time I entered my twenties, I knew a few things for certain: I was going to be an editor and a writer, and someday I would meet my life partner. Sure enough, my work as an editorial intern at a metropolitan newspaper and editor in chief of my college newspaper helped me land my first job as an editor at a national art magazine, where I was working when I began dating my future wife.

Maria proposed four years later on February 29, 2008, one day shy of my thirtieth birthday, in Central Park. Elated, I accepted immediately. Upon our return to Atlanta, I went to the bookstore, one of my favorite places, and began opening books about wedding planning. What I discovered was all "bride and groom": none of the descriptions even applied to Maria and me. Sure, we could *imagine* our place in that book, but the language excluded us. Some wedding guides even had cheerful paragraphs devoted to same-sex "commitment ceremonies" and "civil unions"—phrases that I loathe. "Look, you too can have a ceremony," these authors implied. "Just take all of what I have written here, do the mental gymnastics in your own head about how it applies to you, and go forth with absolutely no confusion or feelings of exclusion. Now let's get back to what happens when a groom makes the toast and his bride may or may not speak . . . " Wedding magazines provided much of the same. I hoped that I would find even one or two mentions of gay or lesbian weddings, but save for the incredibly rare same-sex celebrity wedding, Maria and I were alone in planning our wedding.

Even when we took our search online, we found only a few outdated and rarely updated websites and more obscure gay- or lesbian-specific books, but they didn't speak to us. These well-meaning resources also didn't reflect the understanding that nonheterosexuals include many people who are neither a gay cisgender man nor a lesbian cisgender woman. The LGBTQ+ community is multifaceted, and we didn't yet have full representation in the wedding world. Maria and I were a young, vibrant, and modern couple who needed a wedding resource that simply wasn't available. We wanted something tailored, something true, something made just for us—and it didn't exist.

My heart broke into pieces over this. I felt crushed, forgotten, and unimportant. It felt like my wedding wasn't as good as those of my straight friends. To me, just because same-sex marriages hadn't yet been legally recognized across the country didn't mean that we couldn't have a wedding and be ceremonially married. We weren't going to take second or third rank as citizens by walking up to a separate water fountain and using different terms such as "commitment ceremony." That simply wasn't an option for someone who'd grown up dreaming of her wedding.

I soon found out that the wedding industry could be equally homophobic. I called and emailed wedding vendors with the hope that they could deliver the exquisite services described on their websites or in their magazine ads, only to be hurt and confused when they emailed me back saying they didn't do gay weddings but with Jesus's blessing they might be able to, or when they went silent during a phone call, or, perhaps worse, when they never returned my calls and emails. This experience bothered Maria and me so much that we decided to do

something about it to ensure that other couples like us could avoid feeling excluded.

As soon as our plane landed back on American soil, delivering us from our blissful Caribbean honeymoon on the equality-minded island of Saint Martin, Maria and I got to work—she as the graphic designer and web developer, and me as the writer and editor. We created *Equally Wed,* an online wedding magazine for the modern LGBTQ+ couple. We launched equallywed .com in March 2010, and the world went wild for it. Okay, that's not quite true, but we quickly had a lengthy print feature in the *New York Times,* spots on CNN, and plenty of other media coverage that I'm forever grateful for.

And the LGBTQ+ community reacted with love and gratitude that warmed my heart. Our main purposes were to visually represent modern LGBTQ+ couples getting married, to validate those marriages, to support marriage equality by showcasing the normalcy of these weddings, and to promote the love and equal protection under the law that LGBTQ+ couples deserve. We also wanted to connect LGBTQ+ near-lyweds with equality-minded wedding professionals, a term I coined after working with thousands of vendors who really care about the LGBTQ+ community.

After marriage equality became a federal reality with the 5–4 Supreme Court decision striking down same-sex marriage bans, on June 26, 2015—five years after *Equally Wed* was born—our readership grew significantly. But challenges remain and acceptance in society is far from universal. Much of the wedding industry, which includes media, vendors, and venues, is still learning what it means to be truly equality-minded and only slowly understanding that it has been locked into a heteronormative worldview that isn't everyone's worldview. We all have the right to marriage and to be treated as first-class citizens while we plan our weddings.

The idea for a wedding book for LGBTQ+ couples has been running through my brain for quite some time, but I didn't summon the courage to find a publisher until after the 2015 Supreme Court decision. I knew deep down that everyone deserves a gender-neutral wedding book with which to plan their wedding, whether they're transgender, nonbinary, genderqueer, gender nonconforming, gender fluid, intersex, agender, intergender, lesbian, gay, bisexual, pansexual, queer, or simply label-free. Though the LGBTQ+ community has existed since the beginning of time, we are still fighting for visibility. *Equally Wed* won't allow for our erasure in the wedding world. We're here, we're queer, and we want to get married too.

PREFACE

HOW TO USE THIS BOOK

Wedding planning can be an arduous task that leaves you stressed out over what feels like the need to make a million decisions simultaneously. But if you go at your own pace and give yourself enough lead time, you can actually enjoy the process. This comprehensive wedding planning book is here to guide you through all your tasks as well as lift you up with moral support. We are in this together!

To help you on your path to the altar, I've laid out the tasks to consider in the timeline that works best for most people planning their wedding. While you're reading, feel free to skip ahead, write in the margins, use page stickers to identify what means the most to you, highlight passages for your spouse-to-be, or read it straight through. I also think it would be helpful for your vendors and even key family members to have their own copy of *Equally Wed*, as it's a rich trove of information and perspectives that they may not be familiar with. The more informed everyone involved in your wedding is, the better an experience you will have planning one of the most important days of your life.

Throughout the book, you'll discover what some equallywed.com readers have learned in their own wedding planning process, hear questions we had from other nearlyweds before we published this book, receive advice from some of my favorite equality-minded wedding professionals, and see a few love notes scattered throughout from yours truly.

A WORD TO THE WISE

As the author of *Equally Wed* and the cofounder of the *Equally Wed* website, I recognize perhaps more than some how important words, names, labels, and boxes are—whether it's a matter of usage or avoidance. Gender is a complex and fluid continuum. One of the reasons there was a need for a book like *Equally Wed* was to finally break the mold of the heteronormative terms "bride" and "groom" used in wedding books.

Even other books that mention same-sex weddings often call two female-bodied people getting married two "brides," even though that term isn't universally appropriate in the LGBTQ+ wedding community. By the same token, not all male-bodied people want to be referred to as a "groom." Social constructs are just that: a worldview built by society. People are complex, no matter what our gender identity is or who we fall in love with. More appropriate labels, terms, and words to describe people in our community are certain to be as varied as the community itself. The goal of *Equally Wed* has always been to provide a safe, informative, and inspirational place in which to plan your wedding where your identity is not only validated but valued.

In my experience, most LGBTQ+ people have a certain vocabulary they use to define themselves. Here I've outlined some of the more frequently used terms you'll find in this guide. You might not have seen them before, or be only vaguely familiar with them. Keep in mind that the words you feel most comfortable with do not dictate what you wear or the rituals you practice on your wedding day. For example, a desire to call yourself a groom does not exclude you from being able to carry a bouquet if that's your wish.

LGBTQ+ WEDDING LEXICON

- **Bach party:** A bach (pronounced "batch") party is the gender-neutral term for a bachelor or bachelorette party.
- **Bridal:** The word "bridal" refers to anything related to the marriage and the festive celebrations around it, and its roots are actually gender-neutral. My usage of the word in these pages is always in the gender-neutral sense.

- **Bride:** Anyone can be a bride, no matter their gender identity or orientation. This word is one that you choose for yourself.
- **Bridegroom:** Historically, this term has been used for a man getting married. For modern weddings, anyone can claim this title for themselves.
- **Broom:** "Broom" was coined in 2008 by Maria Palladino, cofounder and publisher of *Equally Wed* and my wife, when we were planning our own wedding. A broom typically presents themself as masculine but prefers this combination of the words "bride" and "groom" rather than "groom."
- **Celebrant:** A gender-neutral term for both a person getting married and the person who performs the marriage ceremony.
- **Cisgender:** The term for someone who identifies as the gender of the body they were born in.
- **Equality-minded wedding professionals:** A trademarked term I created for people and businesses that are cognizant and respectful of varying worldviews and aren't restricted by homogeny. Within the wedding industry, this includes being mindful and respectful of the LGBTQ+ community's specific needs.
- **Gender nonconforming:** The term for someone who does not adhere to stereotypes or other people's views about how they should look or act based on the female or male gender they were assigned at birth.
- **Genderqueer:** The term for someone who identifies with neither, both, or a combination of male and female genders.
- **Gender variant:** Someone whose gender is varied, either in a fluid or a static way.
- **Gride:** A combination of the words "groom" and "bride."
- **Groom:** Anyone can be a groom, no matter their gender identity or orientation. This word is one that you choose for yourself. Grooms can wear anything.
- **Group marriage:** Group marriage is a term applied when more than two people enter into a marriage. While polyamory isn't directly addressed in *Equally Wed*, polyamorous members of the LGBTQ+

community who are planning weddings to multiple partners are welcome here and encouraged to apply any or all of the ideas and guidelines suggested in these pages.

- **Intergender:** This is the term for a person whose gender identity is between genders or a combination of genders.
- **Marrier:** A gender-neutral term for a person getting married or the person who performs the marriage ceremony.
- **Nearlywed:** A gender-neutral term for a person engaged to be married.
- **Nonbinary:** A term for someone who identifies as any gender outside of the male/female binary.
- **They:** This book uses "they" as a singular pronoun, which covers men, women, gender fluid, transgender, and gender-nonconforming individuals. "They" instead of "he or she" has been used in news outlets such as the *Washington Post* and the *Wall Street Journal,* and in fact, it's usage is nothing new. "They" has been used as a singular pronoun for at least seven centuries, appearing in the work of writers from Chaucer to Shakespeare to Jane Austen.
- **Wedding:** A wedding is a wedding is a wedding is a wedding. Regardless of legal standing in your hometown or abroad, your marriage ceremony is about coming together and committing your hearts and lives to one another. I hope marriage equality is one day a global reality. But your wedding isn't any less valid just because a government or society doesn't yet recognize you as equal citizens. You are equal to every other human on this planet, and your love matters.
- **Wedding party:** The terms for your wedding attendants and helpers are endless. I explore name possibilities more on page 26, but there are no rules for how you affectionately name the beloved attendants who stand up for you on your wedding day. Besides, rules are meant to be broken.

Part One

GETTING STARTED

CHAPTER ONE

SHARING YOUR JOY

Congratulations, you're betrothed! Being engaged to your beloved is a thrilling feeling, and it's natural to want to jump straight into the details that interest you most.

In the next chapter, we'll dive into an overview of the timeline, the five most critical decisions to make first, and where to begin in the planning. But if you're like most newly engaged people, you'll want to share the happy news before you start planning.

Before you broadcast the news of your engagement on every social media channel, first take some time to savor this exceptional information with your partner, even if it's only an hour of just the two of you dancing on your happy clouds before you launch the publicity campaign.

THE ANNOUNCEMENT

Once you're ready to share the news, who should you tell first? If you have a good relationship with your parents, start with them. It's historically an honored tradition to reach out to the parents first to reveal that they'll be getting an official new family member before they catch wind of the news secondhand, which can cause unwanted grumbles and hurt feelings. Next, tell your children if you have them, as is the

Many LGBTQ+ couples propose to one another, often on different days—even different months or years. Should you wait to announce your engagement until you've both said "yes"? The short answer is: not necessarily. If partner A proposes in March, partner B might not want to alert partner A that they also have a proposal planned. If this is the case, go ahead and announce and celebrate your engagement in whatever fashion you'd like. Then, when partner B does propose, announce it again. Just be prepared for a calmer celebration this time around, especially from the cisgender heterosexual crowd, who may not understand this LGBTQ+ tradition.

case for a significant number of LGBTQ+ couples—or it was before federal marriage equality. (That stat might start dropping off now that family formation is more likely to happen after legal marriage.) Get the little ones in on the celebration early, especially if you're blending families. Being involved will help them feel more at ease with the coming transition in their lives, such as new siblings, a new stepparent, and possibly a new home.

Close friends should also be contacted before you post a status update or change your relationship status. However, heed this warning: now, at the height of your happiness, be careful not to promise anything to anyone. This isn't a good time to ask people to be involved in—or even to come to—your wedding. Now is the time to simply bask in the glow of being engaged. The rest will come soon enough, and later you'll want to make those decisions carefully. If you make promises while you're floating on cloud nine, you may be full of regret and wondering how to back out of those commitments once you come back down to the world of reason.

With the first announcements to family and close friends out of the way, it's time to consider how you'll tell everyone else. If you're like a lot of people, you're itching to jump on social media and share ring photos and tell the world you're engaged. Or maybe you're more inclined to share your news in the traditional way. What follows are some things to keep in mind, whichever approach you take.

THE SOCIAL MEDIA BLITZ • Do it! Post status updates and photos galore about your giddiness. You can be ever so clever with this step, so have fun! The most basic way to do it—and the sneakiest—is to do nothing but change your Facebook relationship status to "engaged," making sure you allow that status to go into your newsfeed. Simple, yes. Significant, absolutely. Get ready for the ensuing excitement of those who notice!

Want to up your social media cred while sharing the incredibly happy news? Take a cue from your own personality, and your partner's, and get creative with some of these ideas:

1. **If you're on social media 24/7:** Make a meme of a selfie with your cute face(s) and your ring-decorated hand(s). Use a font-based app to type over it with a message such as "I said yes!" or "We're getting hitched!" Post away! On Instagram and Tumblr, gain more visibility and community support with hashtags commonly used in the LGBTQ+ wedding community, such as #LGBTQweddings, #hesaidyes, #twobrides, #twogrooms, #equallywed, #gaywedding, #loveislove, #lovewins, and #howsheasked.

2. **Have young kids?** Photograph them holding up a sign about the upcoming nuptials, à la "My parents are tying the knot!" Or, if you each have children from previous relationships, photograph them together holding up a sign that reads "Our families are becoming one."

3. **Use pet photos for irresistible cuteness overload.** If you're planning on including your furry friend in your wedding ceremony,

it will be even more meaningful if you post an imaginative photo of your pet sharing the news of the engagement for you. Try "Bow to the wow: My humans are engaged!"

Proper wedding etiquette insists that only those who will be invited wedding guests should be sent an engagement announcement or invited to the engagement party.

THE TRADITIONAL APPROACH • If you're the type who prefers handwritten letters and might even still make landline calls instead of communicating solely through texts, tweets, and status updates, consider staying true to yourself by announcing your engagement in a similar fashion.

1. **Putting it in writing:** The tradition of the printed engagement announcement is often overlooked these days, but it's one that is always relished and appreciated. Printed announcements are especially nice if you're not having your wedding within the next two years. If you decide to mail printed engagement announcements, keep the message simple and to the point. For example, "Erin Johnson and Rachel Reynolds are pleased to announce their engagement." Include the date of your engagement, but don't hint at a wedding date or season, a location, or colors. All of your ideas about the wedding are subject to the schedules and availability of your venue and vendors.

2. **A surprise party:** Invite your loved ones to a gathering at your home or a restaurant and announce your engagement to them in person. It can feel a little more genuine to be celebrated in person rather than through likes and shares!

3. **News you can use:** Couples still put their engagement announcements in the newspaper, and now that same-sex marriage is federally recognized, most media outlets are happy to include the news. But they aren't all so inclusive. Call ahead to see what your city rag's policies are. Better yet, have a friend make the call for you

so your heart isn't broken by devastating discrimination. If you do make the cut and your announcement is published, buy copies of the paper for yourself, for your grandparents, and for saving in a frame or a scrapbook. It's a priceless heirloom for future generations, and even more significant for the LGBTQ+ community, as there was a time not too long ago when a newspaper announcement of an LGBTQ+ wedding wasn't allowed at all.

INQUIRING MINDS DON'T NEED TO KNOW

People are naturally going to pummel you with questions about when the wedding will be and whether they will be getting an invitation. This can feel invasive and surprising. You just got engaged, so it's likely that no details are firm except for who you're marrying. But don't worry. You don't have to have any plans yet (and most people don't at this stage). Try to be diplomatic in your response while carving out breathing room where you and your fiancé can revel solely in your engagement. Try this response to well-meaning busybodies: "We haven't started planning yet. We're enjoying our new engagement."

Others won't ask questions but will simply begin making suggestions, even if you aren't asking for advice. They'll bring up their coworker's best friend who had a destination wedding and how they thought it was the most selfish thing in the world. Or they'll start telling you about what they learned from their own wedding. All of this can be interesting—and may be helpful. But right now it's probably just overwhelming. Politely nod and say you've got it covered. Most people will get the hint that you're not jumping to get into the wedding details just yet.

IT'S NOT ALL ROSES AND CHAMPAGNE

You're engaged and ready to celebrate. And why wouldn't everyone want to join in? You know why. Unfortunately, our community doesn't always get the jubilant response from family, coworkers, and others who are in our lives for one unavoidable reason or another. Homophobia and transphobia affect millions of people in communities around the world. You may be asked why you need to go public with your love life. Families who've accepted your sexual orientation and/or your gender identity still might not want the rest of the family to know; a wedding would put a glaring spotlight on what they would prefer to remain a mystery. Or you might not even be able to tell your family you're engaged for fear of complete abandonment.

Families and other formal relationships can be complicated, and there's no magic pill or therapy session to get everybody over to your side—the "love is love" side. But your relationship matters, and you deserve the ultimate love and happiness. You deserve warmth and excitement. If you have friends who are more like family to you, lean on them during this stage. Ask for hugs if you want some. Tell your friends how much their presence matters to you. Let them love on you and celebrate this exciting time in your lives.

Dealing with homophobia and transphobia is incredibly difficult. Some couples have no contact at all with their families of origin for this reason. But if you do, and you wish to let your family know of your engagement even though the reception might not be supportive, here's some encouragement and advice to help you through this step:

1. You matter. Your partner matters. Your relationship is stronger than any force or any person trying to pull it down.

2. You don't have to suffer for the sake of a bloodline. If your family members are becoming verbally aggressive with you, practice self-care and step away for as long as you need.

3. Standing up for yourself is important. Being out and proud is admirable. But taking care of your mental health is everything. So back to that taking-a-break thing. If you need it, do it.

If it's not your family but your partner's family being hurtful, either by making cruel comments or by icing you out, support your spouse-to-be in the same ways you always have, but step it up a notch. Bring your sweetheart flowers and a note detailing how they'll always have you as their family. The feelings of abandonment are real, but knowing that they have you by their side is likely to provide them with some feeling of safety and comfort.

If your family's attitude is questionable but not heinous, give them some time. They may need a period of adjustment to the idea of you marrying someone of the same gender, a trans person, or someone with no gender identification. Let them know you're looking forward to talking with them more when they're comfortable. Then step back a little—but not so far away that they feel like they can't reach out when they're feeling more stable in their support for you and your beloved.

Let your family know that your plans to marry are not going to change. Make sure you tell them how important it feels to have their support for your wedding.

Take the high road. Speak respectfully and with a kind tone. Talk in "I feel" statements. For example, rather than saying, "You're not happy for me," say, "I feel like you're not happy for me." An "I feel" statement, by automatically switching the tone from accusation to explanation of what's going on with you emotionally, is more likely to be followed by open discussions—and solutions.

YOUR WEDDING, YOUR WAY (SERIOUSLY)

Marriage is defined as two (or more) adults committing their lives to one another. Though marriage is about partnership and commitment, society has an extensive history of placing gender stereotypes on marriage and weddings. Some LGBTQ+ celebrants identify as brides and grooms. However, these heteronormative terms don't encompass all people getting married. You don't need to play along, unless you enjoy these terms. If you do, feel free to embrace them as your own while planning your wedding. If you feel strongly about using alternative language, share your preferred terms with your family, friends, and vendors. For more on wording, see the lexicon for LGBTQ+ weddings on page 9.

Alternative Wedding Titles

Don't identify as a bride or a groom? Consider calling yourself one of the following:

Bridegroom: Traditionally defined as a man to be married, "bridegroom" can be redefined for feminine-leaning men, masculine-leaning women, genderqueer, gender-nonconforming, gender-fluid, and nonbinary individuals.

Broom: "Broom" can be either a combination of "bride" and "groom" or a shortened version of "bridegroom."

Celebrant: A person engaged to be married.

Gride: A combination of "groom" and "bride."

Marrier: A person engaged to be married.

Nearlywed: A person engaged to be married.

Partner A and partner B: For contracts with your vendors, the word "partner" demonstrates equality in every way.

Your own name: Simple, right? You don't belong in a box.

No matter if you have a select few who are thrilled for you or an ample supply of cheerleaders in your corner—you're getting married! And that's incredibly special. From my heart to yours, congratulations. Let's get this party started!

THE ENGAGEMENT PARTY

When a couple decides to get married—whether it's through a proposal, or two, or just the result of a conversation—tradition has it that there will be some sort of event to celebrate the engagement. It has no clever name and hardly any rules. It's simply the engagement party. Some LGBTQ+ couples skip the engagement party, but it can be a wonderful opportunity for family and friends to connect (which is precisely why some couples, whose families and friends are quite different

Ask Kirsten

Q: When Tiffany and I got engaged, I thought there would be a big party thrown by my family and friends. But instead, we were greeted by deafening silence. It seemed like hardly anyone was excited for us or wanted to hear about any of our plans. It hurt so much, but more than that, it was confusing. How could this have happened?

A: When people of any orientation become engaged, it can be alienating to their friends and families. Suddenly, the betrothed couple's entire attention is directed toward their wedding plans and their loved ones take a backseat. This is certainly not intentional on the couple's part. Wedding planning can be an intense activity demanding an exorbitant amount of time and energy from the engaged lovebirds.

Sometimes the best approach is to be up front about your feelings. Call each of the people whose silence has hurt you to address your worries. Avoid email. Remember to use "I feel" statements, which will help you stay gracious and humble, rather than accusatory words that put people on edge and make them feel defensive instead of inclined to address your hurt feelings.

from one another, forgo this tradition). The engagement party needn't be awkward or expensive. It's a fun way for all parties involved to get to know each other better because, after all, a wedding is a blending of two families. In the LGBTQ+ community, friends are often just as important as family (and sometimes more so).

Your engagement party can be simple—perhaps a brunch at a friend's home, or cocktails at your favorite restaurant (or even the proposal site!). Or, if your budget allows, you can host a full-on catered fancy fete. Typically, the invitations tell guests that this is an engagement party, unless you're having a surprise announcement party and plan to shock and awe your guests with the news of your engagement. (Fun!)

Many LGBTQ+ couples find that members of their friend and family circles are uncomfortable with the idea of their wedding, especially when the couple is the first LGBTQ+ couple in the community to become engaged. Several things may be going on. They may worry that they're going to say the wrong thing, they may have a religious- or fear-based issue with your upcoming marriage, they may disapprove of your partner, they may have hoped this was only a phase, or they may simply just be too afraid to face their own feelings. Rather than offend you, they may think it's better to avoid you.

LGBTQ+ couples also often encounter LGBTQ+ singles or long-term couples who do not see the value in a wedding. This viewpoint is often held by older LGBTQ+ individuals who see weddings as strictly a heterosexual tradition and therefore assume that anyone having a wedding is trying to "act straight" or pretend they're something they're not.

Seek out answers from these people at your own pace, all the while practicing self-care and remembering that your wedding is ultimately a celebration of happiness and love. Those who are truly happy for you will accept your love and impending marriage without condition.

In classic wedding traditions, the couple's parents arrange the engagement party. These days it's more likely that a close friend or a relative will throw the party; it's still considered poor form to have your own (unless you'll be announcing the engagement). It's like throwing your own birthday bash. If that's something you'd do on your own, then you can do this too. But etiquette experts frown on it because it can appear self-serving and tacky. Plus, it's nice to have someone else honor your upcoming marriage with revelry and merriment.

Engagement party guests naturally assume that they'll be at your wedding—and rightfully so. For this reason, ask your host to invite to the engagement party only people who are going to be invited to the wedding. Don't have your wedding guest list set? Play it safe by shortening the engagement party guest list to the people you are sure will be invited to the wedding—your inner circle of friends and family. It's always better to expand the circle of invitees for the wedding rather than, in a panic, realize later that you need to cut people out of the circle.

Don't expect presents at an engagement celebration. Gifts are not traditionally brought to engagement parties, and if anyone does give you an engagement gift, consider this a high honor. Be sure to accept it graciously and quickly send a follow-up thank-you note.

Tasks to Tackle

- Take time for just the two of you to savor your engagement.
- Plan how you will announce your engagement.
- Make your announcement first to the people you love the most.
- Insure your engagement ring(s).
- If you receive engagement presents, send prompt thank-you notes.
- Take a deep breath. It's wedding planning time!

CHAPTER TWO

TIME MANAGE-MENT, THE ORDER OF BUSINESS, AND ORGANIZATION

Mastering wedding planning involves maintaining all details, prioritizing tasks, and knowing what you want. So how do you go from "I'm engaged!" to "I've got this wedding planned like a boss"?

Start by learning about everything that needs to be done and understanding the interdependence of your decisions. An intense and comprehensive timeline is provided at the end of this book that you can follow, but first, here are the critical elements you'll need to consider: budget, date, guest count, and venue. These four details are dependent on each other. Your budget will dictate what venue you can afford and how many people you can entertain at your reception. Your venue's available dates will determine your wedding date options. Your venue will have a maximum guest capacity—and possibly a minimum—so a lengthy list of people you simply must invite may rule out certain venues. If you're committed to a particular wedding date, then you'll have to find a venue that's available at that time. And then that decision circles back to your budget. See why it's important to get a handle on these four things?

But what about everything else, you might be asking? The decor, the people involved, what you'll wear—it's all important. Imagine your wedding as a certain room in your home—say, the bedroom. In your bedroom, the essential elements are a bed, a dresser, maybe a lamp, and a nightstand. It's smart to purchase these items before you decide on anything else. After all, you need a bed to put the mattress on in order to go to the next step. Once you get these items arranged, then you can concentrate on styling the room. Similarly, the basic building blocks of your wedding are where, when, who, and how much. Once you decide on these foundational aspects, you can go forth with all the details such as what you'll wear, how you'll decorate, what you'll serve, what kind of music you want, and more.

Booking vendors is one of the next big tasks, but they'll ask you about all these elements before they will commit or even provide a cost estimate. So you can see how you've got to lay the foundation of your wedding.

If you want to use a wedding planner for your entire wedding process, start interviewing planners before booking other vendors—and even your venue. A well-connected planner knows local vendors and can help you negotiate prices as well as review vendor contracts. Turn to page 70 for in-depth advice on hiring and working with wedding planners.

Choosing your wedding party early can help you navigate some tasks as well, such as touring venues or researching hotels. Even naming only your honor attendants right now (a best man/woman/person of honor or a maid/matron/gentleman/person of honor) is a great first step. Waiting on asking others to join your wedding party can be smart if you have no idea if you'll have a small or large wedding, as there might not be enough room at the front of the ceremony space for a gaggle of people.

FIVE CRITICAL WEDDING DECISIONS

1. Decide on the venue(s) for the ceremony and reception, choose a date, estimate the guest count, and come up with a budget.
2. Begin to interview and book the vendors who need the longest lead time—those who need to be booked the longest in advance

and can only accommodate one wedding per day—as well as those who may be your absolute favorites, such as the photographer and videographer.

3. Select your wedding party.
4. Interview and book the florist, the officiant, the DJ or other entertainment, the cake maker, the wedding designer, and the stationer or calligrapher.
5. Start your gift registry.

AN ORGANIZED MIND

Finding a way to keep tabs on your timeline, checklists, budget, vendors, and all of your other decisions might seem daunting at first, but I guarantee that it will make things less stressful along the way. Find an organization system that works best for you, whether that's a three-ring binder organized by color-coded tabs; an Excel document; notes in the margins of this book; an online system such as our equality-minded downloadable worksheets at equallywed.com, which account for LGBTQ+-specific purchases like multiple dresses, suits, bouquets, and engagement rings; a notebook; Google Docs, which allows you to access your documents from anywhere you have WiFi; or an app like Evernote, which doesn't require WiFi to access your cached documents.

Once you've committed to a system, stick with it. Design it with at least four columns: estimated expenditure, actual expenditure, deposit paid, and final bill. You'll be noting payments with a variety of vendors and venues, and it's important to keep track of where your funds are going and what's left to pay.

On another tab or in another section, keep hawklike records on the presents you've received, from the bottle of Champagne a friend brings to dinner to congratulate you both on your engagement all the way to the final gifts coming in a month after your wedding. Make columns for:

1. Gift description
2. Date received
3. The store the gift came from

4. Whether the gift was on your registry (so you can check it off if the giver or customer service associate didn't log it during the purchase)
5. The giver's name and mailing address
6. Whether the mandatory handwritten thank-you note has been signed, sealed, and delivered

Set up a separate wedding email address that both you and your spouse-to-be can access, give it to all your vendors, and respond to them only from this address to avoid confusion. Check it daily. You and your spouse-to-be can also use this email account to save and share links to wedding ideas and inspiration.

Tasks to Tackle

- Consider your budget, date, guest count, and venue.
- Decide if you want to use a wedding planner.
- Choose an organization system.
- Set up a separate wedding email address.

CHAPTER THREE

CREATING THE BUDGET

Your wedding is ultimately a declaration of love and commitment. No dollar amount sums up the value of your marriage. Plenty of wedding media outlets and wedding vendors will work tirelessly to convince you that you absolutely must buy their product or service for your wedding or you'll be making a big mistake. Stay strong and decide for yourself what's important to you and your spouse-to-be, and let all the rest fall away.

Setting your budget early will bring you joy, even if it doesn't seem that way at first. Organization is key, and knowing how much you can spend will keep you reined in. Having a wedding budget is important not only for controlling your spending but also for seeing the whole picture and assessing what else needs to be done. Weddings are an expense—generally a costly one—whether you're on a shoestring budget or planning a lavish affair.

FIRST THINGS FIRST • Are your parents (or other relatives) going to help you with the cost of the wedding? While that source of support used to be expected, modern wedding stats are reporting that only two-thirds of straight couples have help from their parents, and the figure is even less for the LGBTQ+ set. With the recent advent of federal marriage equality, it's becoming quite common for couples who have been together for a decade or even half a century to get married. With older LGBTQ+ couples tying the knot, it's even more rare for families to help out—not because they don't care, but because the couple is financially established.

You may receive very generous and loving offers to help pay for some or all of your wedding. Parents and relatives who can't offer money might try to help out in other ways, such as baking the cake or helping you assemble the invitations, envelopes, and postage.

The people who love you the most will want to be involved somehow, some way, and this is a testimony to their devotion to you. Accept their help graciously, but try not to expect such support of anyone. Wedding traditions are changing for couples of all orientations, and while it's wonderful when families help out, they may decline for a myriad of reasons. Whoever pays for the wedding—in total or in part—will have opinions about the big day and will expect to have their voice heard. Ultimately, the decisions lie with you and your honey, but as a courtesy, genuinely listen to the people who are helping foot the bill for your wedding. This delicate subject should be handled with care, as most people are sensitive about how their money is spent.

Once you've factored in potential contributions from others, sit down with your partner and decide what the two of you can allocate for your big day. What can you afford, and how much do you want to spend? These are two very different questions, and it's best to answer them both as a couple. Take all night and a bottle of wine or your go-to late-night snack to hash it out. If necessary, decide on a longer engagement to give yourselves more time to save funds. I don't recommend using credit cards unless you can pay them off within the first year; being in debt is one of the least romantic ways to begin your marriage.

ALLOCATING FUNDS

By now you should have a rough idea of the total amount you can spend on your wedding. These funds need to cover pre-wedding festivities, wedding attire and jewelry (though presumably not the bling already on your finger and/or your fiancé's), every bill you'll pay for your ceremony and reception, and post-wedding expenses such as the send-off brunch and postage for thank-you notes. Frequently, engagement jewelry and honeymoon costs aren't included in wedding budgets since they're considered pre- and post-wedding elements that aren't directly tied to the wedding. It's up to you whether to include these costs in the financial planning or not.

Before you get in over your head with dreams of a string quartet courting you down the aisle or a wall of roses in the entryway for your wedding, let's discuss the wedding budget in full, with a breakdown of what your money may be covering. Keep in mind that you'll probably overspend in some areas and (maybe!) spend a little less in other areas. Perhaps you've allocated $3,000 for flowers, but then your Aunt Julie offers to source the flowers wholesale and create the arrangements herself. Or you discover a fabulous wedding baker who costs a minor fortune, but you simply must have that person design your wedding cake. Adjustments like these happen all the time. If you're a strict type-A personality, go ahead and plan for wedding budget fluctuations

Ask Kirsten

Q: My parents paid for my three sisters' weddings, and now I'm getting married to the man of my dreams. Because I'm a man, my parents don't think they should have to pay for my wedding too. My feelings are hurt, and I don't know what to do. Please help!

A: In heterosexual weddings of yore, the bride's parents did traditionally foot the bill for the entire wedding, while the groom's parents paid for the transportation, officiant, alcohol, and rehearsal dinner, as well as the bride's flowers. But times have changed. In modern practice, whoever can help is welcome to do so, but no one except the couple is responsible for the cost of the wedding.

That being said, it's understandable that your feelings are hurt. Try sitting down with your parents without your fiancé or your sisters around and telling them what you just told me. Let them know that you don't expect any financial handouts, but that it would mean the world to you if they would treat your wedding as an event just as important to them as your sisters' weddings.

to minimize the inevitable stress. And if you can allot an emergency fund for splurges and catastrophic incidents, all the better. The more relaxed you feel during the entire wedding planning process, the more fun it will be.

Another way to feel comfortable with your wedding budget is to go ahead at this point and research the cost of the vendors and venues you're considering. You might be in for some sticker shock, but it's better to absorb it now at the start of the process. Keep in mind that wedding costs vary significantly from state to state. The higher the cost of living in a region, the more expensive overall services and rental fees tend to be as well. Wedding costs are also incredibly dependent on experience and quality. The longer a person has been in the business, the higher their fees usually are (though, as in everything in life, a high price tag doesn't automatically translate into high quality).

To build out your wedding budget, first consider all of the possible elements of a wedding. You may want only a few of them or all of them, depending on your wedding style. Most of the elements are present in a typical wedding, but your wedding is not a cookie-cutter replica of all the weddings that came before yours, and neither is your budget. The following list includes all the elements of a wedding that typically need to be accounted for in a budget, but your own wedding budget will be specific and tailored to where you plan to allocate your funds.

- After-party
- Attendant gifts
- Attire for attendants
- Bartender(s)
- Bouquets
- Boutonnieres
- Cake
- Catering
- Ceremony venue rental fee
- DJ, musician, and/or band
- Favors
- Florist
- Gifts for anyone who gave money
- Gown(s)
- Hair and makeup
- Invitations
- Liquor
- Lodging
- Marriage license
- Morning-after brunch
- Officiant fee
- Partner gifts
- Photographer
- Planner
- Postage
- Reception decor and rentals
- Reception venue rental fee
- Rehearsal dinner
- Save-the-dates
- Shoes
- Stationery and paper goods
- Suit(s)
- Tips
- Travel to and from the wedding
- Videographer
- Wedding app
- Wedding rings
- Wedding website
- Welcome bags
- Welcome party

Remember, you don't have to have everything on this list. It's important to choose what you want and let the other elements fall by the wayside. For now, let's assume that your wedding will include most of these elements and that funds will need to be allocated to each one.

There's no perfect one-size-fits-all budget calculator for every couple, but on average the reception costs the most money. From there, prioritizing what you spend money on is entirely up to you. Some couples feel that wedding photography deserves as much as one-fourth of the wedding funds, while others want the reception to be the best party of the century and will spare no expense to make sure that happens, with a live band, hired dancers, and all types of fun to keep the merriment going.

The wedding budget guideline on the next page will help you make the most of your wedding budget. Take the entire amount you've decided on for your wedding spending and start playing with how you're going to divide it up. Factor in adjustments based on your own priorities. One couple's dream venue is another couple's must-have award-winning photographer. Adjust your budget accordingly.

A GUIDE TO TIPPING VENDORS

Gratuity is a way of saying thanks to hired employees who go above and beyond, but it's also just as expected as tipping your server at a restaurant. When you add up all the tips you're going to give to service providers in your wedding, the total could make a real dent in your wedding budget. So it's important to factor into your budget the tips you're likely to be doling out for satisfactory service and especially for service that exceeds your expectations.

The following lists industry-standard gratuity percentages, though how much you give is discretionary. If someone has exceeded your expectations, feel free to give them extra or send a handwritten note after your wedding. Assign someone discerning and trustworthy

A Typical Wedding Budget Guideline

Attire 6%

Ceremony music 2%

Ceremony site 2%

Favors 1%

Flowers 6%

Hair and makeup 2%

Hotels/lodging 3%

Invitations and
    announcements 3%

Parking and transportation 2%

Photography 11%

Reception (venue, catering,
    and rentals) 40%

Reception music and
    entertainment 7%

Rehearsal dinner 6%

Videography 4%

Wedding rings 5%

to hand out tips on the day the service is provided. (Create labeled envelopes of cash ahead of time.) Before giving anyone a tip, check each vendor contract to make sure gratuities aren't built in.

- **Bartenders:** Either $20 per hour per person or 10% of the total liquor bill (if you didn't supply the alcohol)
- **Catering manager, banquet captain, and/or maître d':** $200–$300
- **Chef:** $100–$200
- **Coat check:** $1–$2 per guest
- **Deliveries and setup staff:** $5–$10 per person setting up your cake, tent, floor, etc.
- **DJ or bands:** $20–$25 per musician; $50–$150 for DJs
- **Hair and makeup:** 15–25% of the total service bill
- **Musicians:** $15–$20 per musician
- **Officiant:** $50–$100 or a personal gift. (Tipping a hired officiant

is appreciated; the officiant provided by a religious institution is "tipped" by making a donation to the church or synagogue.)

- **Photographer**: $50–$200 (not expected and purely optional)
- **Transportation**: 15%
- **Videographer**: $50–$200 (not expected and purely optional)
- **Waiters**: $20 or $30 per waiter
- **Wedding planner**: 10–20% of their fee or a personal gift. (Consider digitally transmitting high-resolution wedding photos to the planner for their portfolio as a gift.)

Tasks to Tackle

- Commit to mindful spending while also enjoying yourself.
- Consider setting up a separate bank account for wedding funds.
- Decide which parts of the wedding are most important to you.
- Figure out who's paying.
- Get organized with a digital or physical notebook.
- If necessary, make a plan to start saving for your wedding.
- Set a wedding budget.

CHAPTER FOUR

BE OUR GUEST!

A wedding only legally needs one witness beyond the offici-ant and the couple, but you'll probably want more people to witness this enormous commitment you're making. The number of guests will dictate the cost of just about everything for your wedding, from chair rentals to food, and your venue and budget typically dictate the number of guests you can have. An outdoor wedding at your city's botanical garden might allow only 50 guests, and the hotel ballroom you've been enamored with might have not only a maximum of 500 but also a minimum. That being said, I think it's also clever to work the math in reverse: who do you want at your wedding, and what venue and level of spending would it take to bring them all together? To produce a well-orchestrated event you'll need to consider how cohesively all of these aspects can work together, as well as what your priorities are.

Once you have a rough idea of how many guests can be accom-modated by both your wedding and reception venues, it's time to get to work on the invitation list. Together with your partner, create one list of those friends and family members who absolutely must receive an invitation. Does this number match up at all with guest count requirements of your weddings venues? If the list cannot be amended accordingly, you may need to consider changing your venues.

HOW MANY GUESTS SHOULD YOU INVITE?

Some experts suggest inviting 20% more guests than your budget or venue allows for, with the expectation that not everyone invited will be able to attend. But what if everyone invited accepts your invitation? If you can't afford to host them all, or could do so only in a bigger venue, don't risk it. Invite who you want, but only as many as you can manage.

THE B LIST

Compiling a wedding guest B list gives you a backup plan: you'll invite some from this group of people you're on the fence about only if a certain number of guests from your A list decline. The only way you can get away with this is by sending out invitations super-early (more than three months out), so that you'll start receiving responses earlier. Also, don't put anyone on your B list who is friends with someone on your A list. If anyone discovers they were on the B list, their feelings will rightly be hurt and your relationship could truly suffer.

BUILDING YOUR GUEST LIST

FINANCIAL CONTRIBUTORS' OPINIONS • Anyone paying for some or all of your wedding is probably going to voice an opinion about your guest list. This doesn't mean you have to honor specific requests, but if it's important to your financial supporter to invite their best friend, or a neighbor from your childhood, see if you can make it happen. Even though technically your wedding is your big day, it's also about bringing all your loved ones together as a family.

It's less common to have family members offering to pay for any or all of an LGBTQ+ wedding, so when they do, it can feel as if their opinions hold more weight. Some couples allow contributing parents or grandparents to invite a certain number of guests, such as ten or twenty—or perhaps fifty if it's an incredibly large wedding. Ideally, at the end of the day, you feel warmly about all of the people who will attend your wedding. But often certain concessions have to be made.

Q: My neighbor has been dropping hints about wanting an invitation to my wedding ever since I mentioned our engagement to her. She's a bit of a hermit, with no real friends to speak of, so I'd feel guilty if I didn't invite her. But she's not really someone I want to have there—she's a bit obnoxious and tells crude jokes. How do I handle this?

a: Your discomfort in this situation is completely understandable. If you aren't going to invite this neighbor, try to remain neutral and maintain harmony with her, since you're likely to continue seeing her regularly after your wedding unless you and your new spouse are planning on moving soon. If your neighbor doesn't come right out and ask if she can come, you're not obligated to respond to the hints. However, you could say politely, in a similarly hinting manner, something like, "We wish we could afford to invite everyone we know, but our budget doesn't allow for it."

Just make sure you're standing up for what really matters to you. Your comfort is vital to reduce your stress levels.

THE PLUS-ONE QUESTION • Should you allow single wedding guests to bring a date? It's a common courtesy if your budget allows for it, but you're under no obligation to invite plus-ones. Etiquette dictates that you invite the spouse, partner, fiancé(e), or significant other of any guest, even if you haven't met them. But after that, see what your budget and head count can handle.

CHILDREN • Now is the time to decide if any children will be invited to or included in your ceremony. Much of this decision-making will depend on how involved you are with the children of your family and friends, or if you have children of your own. Children can add a hopeful innocence and playful mirth to weddings, charming guests with their lovely presence and serving as a symbol of family and fertility. But not everyone wants children at their wedding, as they can distract the adult guests and depending on their age they require extra care. For advice on how to indicate whether children are welcome at your wedding, see page 62.

> Having trouble whittling down your guest list? Ask yourself: will this person be in our lives in five years?

THE HOMOPHOBIC OR TRANSPHOBIC RELATIVE • You and your partner will need to do some serious soul-searching as you try to decide whether to invite a homophobic or transphobic relative. Obviously, you'd never want someone at your wedding who wishes you ill. But you and your partner are likely to have at least one family member—if not dozens—who doesn't believe you should be getting married at all or, at the very least, gives you the "I'm so uncomfortable with your sexual orientation or gender presentation" vibe whenever you see them. So why would you invite someone like this to witness you entering into a covenant of marriage?

Well, in the first place, you may love this relative unconditionally despite their conditional love for you. Perhaps it would break your heart if they didn't come to your wedding and you can't bear to not at least invite them, in the hope that their viewpoint will change once they see how real your commitment is. Frequently, it is the relatives who act indifferent to, or even offended by, an LGBTQ+ family member's relationship who bawl with happy tears at the wedding, overcome with emotion for the love they've witnessed. Sometimes you really do have to see it to believe it: the epiphany that all love is equal, no matter a person's gender, happens at LGBTQ+ weddings every weekend around the world. Weddings can be a lovely opportunity for changing hearts and opening minds.

REMEMBERING THE ENGAGEMENT PARTY • Anyone invited to any of your pre-wedding parties—including engagement parties,

Save the Date!

Save-the-date announcements should be sent out at least six months before the wedding. Make sure your guest list is solid before these go out: it's a terrible feeling to receive a save-the-date card but then never get the invitation.

What's included on a save-the-date (or STD, as they're often referred to in the wedding world)? Your names, the wedding date (including the year), the city and state where you'll be tying the knot, and, if you'd like, your wedding website. Design options run the gamut from cute postcards to photo magnets. Digital STDs are absolutely acceptable and increasingly common. Just make sure they go directly to your intended guests' inboxes, since socially shared wedding announcements will hurt the feelings of those excluded. Also, if you intend to invite an elderly relative or a friend living off the grid, now's the perfect time to pick up the phone or pen a handwritten note.

showers, bach parties, and rehearsal dinners—should also be invited to the wedding. Even if you were not in charge of the guest list for an engagement party or a shower, or the parties were held before the wedding guest list was formalized, you should add these guests to your wedding invitation list. Exceptions to this rule are the guests at showers hosted by coworkers and the guests at showers held by your parents in a town far away, who probably wouldn't be able to travel to your wedding.

DESTINATION WEDDING GUESTS • It's important to finalize your guest list early if you're having a destination wedding. Your guests will need to consider the additional costs and time involved in traveling, so it's a generous courtesy to let them know as soon as possible where and when you'll be getting married. Your guest list for a destination wedding is likely to be shorter than it would be for a local wedding.

Expect only family and close friends to attend, but do still invite relatives who you know might not be able to travel, such as elderly grandparents, so they'll feel included. And keep in mind that not all who are invited will be able to attend, either because the travel costs are prohibitive or they cannot get the necessary time off from work. Be prepared to handle these conversations and declinations with grace. If there is someone who you want to be there but who cannot afford the flight, you may privately offer to pay for their airfare. Keep in mind that the couple typically pays for lodging, but not transportation, for the wedding party.

THE WEDDING PARTY

After you decide on the major details, it's time to think about your wedding party. Do you want attendants? If so, how many would you like to have? Don't wait too long to ask them, as their help will be much appreciated during the planning process.

HONOR ATTENDANTS • Each partner can choose someone to whom they're especially close—a sibling, another family member, a close friend—to serve as an honor attendant. This person typically takes on more tasks than the other attendants, such as organizing showers and making sure all attendants have their attire.

ATTENDANTS • Although not required, traditional wedding etiquette recommends inviting siblings to be attendants. If you or your partner don't want your siblings in this role, you could invite them to participate in other special roles, such as giving a reading or managing your guest book.

CHILD ATTENDANTS • Flower attendants are typically younger children, but adults can fill this role, and the same goes for the ring bearer. Children can also serve as junior attendants, wedding gown train holders, or candle lighters. There is no limit to the number of young attendants you may have, but typically these roles are reserved for relatives and the children of especially close friends.

HOW MANY ATTENDANTS? • How many attendants you have is up to you. If your wedding will be an intimate affair in a small venue, you might not want to have twelve attendants. Conversely, only one or two attendants in an enormous space might also look off. Matching numbers on either side isn't as important as making sure all the people you want standing beside you are there.

HANDLING REJECTION

Being an attendant does come with a cost, so if someone tells you they love you dearly but simply cannot afford it, either discreetly offer to assist them with their attire purchase or let them bow out gracefully.

Tasks to Tackle

- Discuss guest list options with your partner and family.
- Decide whether or not children will be invited.
- Expect to call a few folks who forget to RSVP.
- Finalize your guest list.
- Create an organized list of all wedding guests, including mailing addresses and phone numbers.
- Assemble your attendants.

Part Two

ELEMENTS OF THE DAY

CHAPTER FIVE

DATE AND VENUE

The location and timing of your wedding ceremony and reception set the tone for the entire event. Whether you're going for the glitz and glam of a grand ballroom wedding or the easygoing vibe of a beach ceremony with the surf whipping at your hair, whether you're having an evening candlelit dinner reception in a loft or getting married in a backyard wedding filled with wildflowers and seriously good craft brew, every type of venue has its own logistics to consider.

Where your wedding takes place is the foundation for your wedding style, giving it the look and feel of your big day. Take time with your partner to put the pens and paper away and just get dreamy. Close your eyes if you'd like. Imagine what your perfect ceremony looks like. Is it in a church? At a ranch with dusty trails, horses, and a majestic oak tree? On the rooftop of a big hotel with city lights twinkling around you? Just imagine by yourself what you want. Have your partner do the same. Then compare notes.

QUESTIONS TO ASK
YOURSELF AND EACH OTHER

- What city should we marry in? Where we live now or in one of our hometowns?
- Should we consider a destination wedding?
- Do we want a small, medium, or large wedding?

- No matter the budget, what percentage of it are we open to spending on a venue? Is it one of our top priorities or just the backdrop?
- Do we want a venue that provides every service so we can sit back and relax, or are we more interested in piecing the wedding elements together with our vendors?
- Are we open to a nontraditional off-site wedding, where we'll have to rent tents, chairs, tables, linens, and even portable restrooms? Or would we rather marry and celebrate at a venue where those items are provided?
- Do we want a small ceremony with no guests and then a large wedding reception?

Much of what you want for your wedding is achievable and a lot more—on any budget. It's not so much a matter of what you can afford and then planning from there—as the wedding industry would have you believe—as of determining your top priorities and then bringing that vision to life.

VENUES

The term "wedding venue" traditionally describes the reception site, but many LGBTQ+ couples choose to have the ceremony and reception take place in the same venue.

TYPES OF VENUES • Almost any space can be transformed into a wedding venue. If you can dream it (and afford it), it can (probably) happen. Here are some of the most common:

Hotel Ballroom • Hotels have almost everything couples could wish for, and all within reach: on-site catering staff, professional-grade kitchens, stocked bars, ample rooms to get ready in, rooms for your guests, in-house wedding planning staff, and, quite often, access to some of your city's premium wedding vendors who know what works best in the venue and how to best achieve your vision.

Hotels are not inexpensive by any means, with their minimums for food and beverage and base cost per guest. However, if you add up every single item you'd have to cart in for your own DIY wedding—chairs, tables, tents, linens, glasses, flatware, portable bathrooms, etc.—you might discover that you'd save more money using a hotel.

Considering that some ballrooms double as convention and meeting spaces, a hotel may need more outside assistance in transforming the space to match your vision. But the right event designer can stage your wildest dream in any room (for a price). If you're considering a hotel wedding, find out if you can bring in your own vendors. Many hotels require that you go through them for food and beverage. And some might insist that you use their florist or other vendors.

House of Worship • Now that the United States offers marriage equality in every state, more houses of worship are allowing same-sex wedding ceremonies. If you opt to have your wedding in a holy space, your venue cost might be lowered significantly.

Unfortunately, there are still fewer churches and synagogues that allow same-sex marriage and more that do not condone it—or forbid it outright. However, if you and your partner are part of a supportive congregation, you already know if your wedding ceremony is going to be allowed in your house of worship. Ask early, however, and make no assumptions: I've met quite a few couples who were stunned and hurt when they asked to have their wedding ceremony in the church they attended as a couple, often for years, and were turned down because of their church's stance on same-sex relationships.

If you opt for a wedding ceremony in your house of worship, you'll probably select another venue for your reception, depending on what your house of worship offers in the way of entertaining space.

Restaurant • Restaurant weddings boast delightful ambiance, delicious food, and built-in decor. Though not considered a true full-service wedding venue, most come equipped with a variety of necessities, from linens, tables, and flatware to bathrooms, a parking plan (maybe even valet), a bar, and a coat-check room. The downside of a restaurant wedding can be the monster expense of having a wedding during normal business hours. To persuade most restaurants to close

service to their clientele, you will need to guarantee the restaurant manager that you'll be spending on food and beverage what the restaurant could make in a night. However, larger restaurants sometimes offer function rooms reserved explicitly for wedding receptions and similar parties so the restaurant may continue serving its regular clientele. In terms of personalization, you might find it harder to bring in your own food vendors for something special, but you could also ask the chef to prepare a dish you want served at the wedding, such as your great-aunt Edna's chicken potpie recipe.

Home or Backyard • Home wedding receptions used to be a staple before the wedding industry became the behemoth that it is today. A simple church wedding and then back to the house for a modest cake and punch. Many couples are returning to this tradition and making it their own for weddings of all sizes—including the ceremony. What's great about home weddings is that you're not paying for a venue, there's no time limit (though check your city's sound ordinance for late-night music), and there's an innate sense of familiarity, whether you gather in your home or a loved one's.

Keep in mind that you'll still have to rent (or borrow) quite a few items to outfit your house wedding, especially if the guest list is larger than thirty people. Expect to outsource linens, tables, chairs, possibly a tent, and at least one posh portable bathroom.

Destination Wedding • Chic and memorable, destination weddings are the modern couple's way of eloping—with guests. Presumably there's a great deal less fuss over a destination wedding, but ask anyone who's planned a destination wedding and they'll tell you how much work it is, potentially including international calls with wedding vendors, a few trips to your location for walk-throughs, the expense of shipping any items from home, wedding attire insurance, additional travel expenses for the wedding trip, and the guilt you may feel asking family and friends to spend their money and use their vacation time to travel to your destination wedding. However, all of this aside, a destination wedding can be a fabulous party, and many couples don't mind the extra work for the opportunity to exchange vows in an exotic locale.

Outdoors • Whether you're having a backyard wedding or getting married out in the middle of nowhere, most everything will need to be brought to the space, since it obviously won't be provided. But the photos with all the gorgeous lighting and natural elements will be worth it! If you are working with an unlimited budget or are willing to pull up your shirtsleeves and work hard, this could be the route for you. However, if worrying about rain ruining your day is going to keep you up night after night, either make peace with having a rain-contingency plan or go for something entirely indoors.

New-Fashioned Wedding Venue • From auction houses and nature parks to city attractions (the zoo, the aquarium, a museum), an art gallery or studio, your college campus, or somewhere completely different, unconventional venues offer an offbeat and fun alternative to more traditional wedding sites.

The Right Venue for You • With all these options, it's best to decide on what key elements you're looking for as you narrow your focus to a few venues. Consider which venue will meet the most of your needs, whether that's a place with accommodations on the grounds or nearby for your guests, the one with the strongest possibility for good photography (good lighting, spectacular scenery, etc.), a one-stop shop where you don't have to research vendors on your own, or a venue with the fewest restrictions on decorating the space.

SETTING THE DATE • Once you have narrowed your venue choices down to your top three, find out about their availability. Then consider the date options they give you before signing any paperwork. Look over last year's calendar in your phone or desk planner. Is one date option also your best friend's birthday weekend? Or a special holiday? Does it fall during a time period when important wedding guests might be unable to show up? If your family is heavily involved in your wedding planning, discuss the options with them to make sure everyone is equally excited about the chosen date.

Of course, if you have a special month and day you're going for (say, your grandparents' wedding anniversary, or the anniversary of your first date, or even, as is the case for many LGBTQ+ couples, the date of your first nonlegal wedding ceremony), don't be afraid to ask the venue for that date. Its availability often depends on how far out you're planning your wedding. The longer your planning period is, the better your chances for booking the venue and vendors of your choice. If you're getting married in an unconventional spot, the chances are much better that your venue will be available on the day you wish.

QUESTIONS FOR WEDDING VENUES BY PHONE OR DURING A SITE VISIT

- Have you ever hosted an LGBTQ+ wedding before? When? Can you connect me with one of the couples for a referral?

- How do you train your employees to be equality-minded? *You can have a super-friendly front-desk person, but just one homophobic waiter or transphobic bathroom attendant can easily create a hostile and hurtful environment. If you have any doubts about this venue's ability and knowledge, make it known that you expect everyone to be professional and welcoming to all of your guests or you will take your business elsewhere.*

- Do you have a place where we can both separately get ready? *Offering only one suite is awfully heteronormative and presumes that only one of you needs and wants space in which to prepare for the marriage ceremony.*

- How many hours are included in the standard rental contract? Can I add more if I wish?

- Is the cost of rental for a ceremony rehearsal included?

- Where can supplies and rentals be loaded in and loaded out?

- Walk us through the potential ceremony and reception setups.
- Do you have a coat check?
- Do you provide valet parking? What are the parking options? Do you offer free or reduced parking for wedding guests?
- Do you offer free WiFi? *You'll need it if you're streaming music.*
- What sort of lighting do you offer? *You may need to bring in your own lighting rentals—be sure this is allowed.*
- What rules do you have about bringing in decor?
- What decor, tables, linens, chairs, etc., do you provide? *Check out these details if you have a chance—what the venue offers might be outdated or just not your style. Make sure you can bring in your own items if you'd like.*
- Is the location subject to a noise ordinance?
- Do you have a set list of vendors we are required to choose from?
- What vendors do you love working with? *Selecting vendors who are familiar with your venue can help the event go more smoothly.*
- Where are your restrooms? Are they wheelchair-accessible? How do you feel about our plan to hang unisex signs on them?
- What equipment do you provide caterers and musicians and what needs to be brought in?
- Is there an additional fee for the electricity used?
- Can we use sparklers for our exit?
- Will there be any other weddings here on our day?
- Ask for a sample contract. *You need to review the contract for potential red flags before getting your heart set on a particular place.*

THE SITE VISIT

After you're satisfied with the answers, it's time to do a site visit. (If you're saving your questions for your visit, don't forget to bring along this list!) A site visit allows you to tour the property, imagine your wedding there, and make sure there's space for all the tables, a bandstand if you want, ample bathrooms, a commercial-grade kitchen for your caterer to work in, etc. Introduce yourself and your partner to anyone you see there and watch for their immediate reaction. You're looking for all employees to be welcoming and kind. If they can't treat you respectfully on a tour, how will they treat you and your guests on your wedding day?

Tasks to Tackle

- Begin researching venues.
- Determine the season in which you want to marry.
- Narrow down your venue search.
- Tour equality-minded venues.
- Review venue contracts carefully. (Feel free to ask for revisions that are important to you, and ask for a final copy with all signatures.)
- Lock in a date with your preferred venue.

CHAPTER SIX

INVITATIONS AND STATIONERY

Soon after the wedding planning gets under way, you'll want to begin researching the stationery suite that will best suit your needs. Whether you're springing for luxurious heavy card stock with each guest's name written in calligraphy or your style is more out-of-the-box meets practical, there's more written communication involved in a wedding than you might be aware of, from the constant flurry of thank-you notes to the wedding invitations, RSVP cards, response envelopes, ceremony programs, and reception menus. Because it's expensive to have to print things twice, wait until your wedding date and venue are set and you have a rough estimate of your guest count before ordering your stationery.

Invitations, which run the gamut from simple printed information on linen paper to foil-pressed trifold cards to digital options, give your guests the first hint of what to expect at your wedding. Let your wedding style lead the way by aiming to convey the theme and overall feeling of your wedding through your selection of paper, style, type-faces, and wording.

Wedding stationery is the wardrobe of paper goods that you'll use during and after your wedding, from invitations, thank-you notes, save-the-date announcements, and place cards to table numbers, wedding programs, reception menus, and reply cards. It's best to go with a consistent design for a cohesive feeling throughout your wedding. If you do mix and match designs, create a flow by using an identical font, logo, or colors throughout. Remaining with the same invitation company will help achieve this look.

Remember to order invitations per household, not per guest. The price difference can be astronomical—and it's just a waste of paper and money.

Start researching your options early, requesting samples from invitation vendors and companies so you can get a feel for the texture and weight of the paper. When placing your order, leave yourself enough time to check everything for misprints and getting a new set if necessary.

INVITATION 101

Begin by sending out your save-the-dates: the informal announcements mailed to everyone on your firm guest list so that they can pencil in your wedding on their calendar. Then your wedding invitations should be sent out between eight and twelve weeks before the wedding. (Add at least another month for destination weddings.) By allowing plenty of time for responses, you'll be able to update your vendors about the guest count.

Also be sure to give yourself plenty of time to assemble the wedding invitations before mailing them out. Translation: order the invitations as soon as your wedding date, time, and venue(s) are firm and contracts have been signed. Remember that you'll need extra time for more elaborate invitations with features such as engraving or letterpress.

Reception information is generally included in the invitation, as well as a reply card for an RSVP. If you're having multiple functions on your wedding weekend and everyone is invited, include an additional printed card with that information. The simplest invitations include (1) a piece of paper with the wedding details (when and where), (2) a reply card, and (3) a pre-addressed, pre-stamped response envelope.

WORDS MATTER

The wording on wedding invitations is an oft-discussed matter. There's a precise and somewhat complex order to a traditionally worded invitation—and then there's the new-fashioned invitation wording of same-sex couples, reflecting feminist principles. Whereas wedding invitations for one bride marrying one groom often use only the bride's first and middle names and the groom's first, middle, and last, modern tradition recognizes that both marrying parties are equal and should be treated as such, even on the invitations. The formalities, structure, and underlying etiquette of invitation wording can make some couples crazy. Just keep in mind the essential message you want to convey: who is getting married, when they're getting married (both date and time), and where they're getting married.

HONORING THE HOST

When you honor the host in your invitation, you're not necessarily referring to the person who's paying for the wedding. In fact, you can honor anyone in these lines, such as grandparents, siblings, aunts, the person who has looked after you since you left home, etc. You can choose to mention your parents and not your partner's. It's your day, so do it your way. The most important message for your guests is when and where to show up!

FORMAL INVITATIONS

There are some formal rules to follow in writing a classic wedding invitation:

- List the hosts first.
- Spell out all the dates and numbers except multi-digit numbers (for example, "Twenty Belle Isle Circle," but "8450 Peachtree Road").
- Use the expression "o'clock" instead of "A.M." or "P.M."
- Abbreviate nothing except social titles, such as Ms., Mr., Mrs., Mx., and Ind.
- Spell out military titles, "Doctor" or "Reverend" used as titles, and "Junior" and "Senior."

- Write in the third-person voice.
- Center the wording except for the RSVP, which is flush left.
- Do not use punctuation unless a phrase, such as the date, requires it ("Saturday, the eleventh of May").

Let's look at these elements of the invitation in a bit more detail.

If any or all of the parents are hosting the wedding, lead with their names. If they are not married to one another, list them on separate lines in alphabetical order to correlate with the celebrants—*not* in order of who contributed the most (or at all). So, if partner A's parents are listed first, then list partner A first when naming the celebrants.

You can use the British spelling of the word "honor" ("honour"), but the American spelling is still considered formal. "[The hosts] request the honour/honor of your presence" is the wording used for a wedding in a house of worship and "the pleasure of your company" is the correct phrase to use for a wedding ceremony held anywhere but a house of worship (even if it's a religious wedding).

If the couple is hosting, there is no need to mention parents or particular family members, but "together with their families" can be added to the couple's names.

For the most formal of invites, you can opt to capitalize every letter, but it's not an absolute requirement. Also, for Jewish wedding invitations, connect the couple's names with "and" (not "to").

The time of the wedding should appear on one line, in all lowercase letters. If your wedding is at six o'clock, the time line should read, "at six o'clock." The time line for weddings held at 6:30 p.m. should read, "at half after six o'clock."

The time line can designate the time of day as "in the morning," "in the afternoon," or "in the evening," but it's not usually necessary, since a wedding held at "six o'clock" is obviously being held in the evening. Denoting the time of day is helpful, however, for weddings held at 8:00, 9:00, or 10:00, since these times could refer to either the morning or the evening.

EXAMPLES OF FORMAL WEDDING INVITATIONS

THE PLEASURE OF YOUR COMPANY IS REQUESTED
AT THE MARRIAGE OF
Ms. RACHEL ELIZABETH GREENE
TO
Ms. KATHERINE BLYTHE WHITNEY
SATURDAY, THE NINTH OF JUNE
TWO THOUSAND EIGHTEEN
AT HALF AFTER SIX O'CLOCK
THE RESORT AT PAWS UP
40060 PAWS UP ROAD
GREENOUGH, MONTANA 59823
RECEPTION TO IMMEDIATELY FOLLOW

Ms. WILLA ANTONIA CARTER AND Ms. OLIVIA ANNE DIETRICH
MR. ROBERT JOHNSON
REQUEST THE HONOR OF YOUR COMPANY
AT THE MARRIAGE OF THEIR DAUGHTER
MARY ELIZABETH DIETRICH
TO
DYLAN HARRIS LOGAN
OF MX. JAMES HARRIS LOGAN AND DOCTOR EVAN ROYCE LOGAN
ON SATURDAY, THE NINTH OF DECEMBER
TWO THOUSAND EIGHTEEN
AT THREE O'CLOCK
SAINT MARK UNITED METHODIST CHURCH
781 PEACHTREE STREET NORTHEAST
ATLANTA, GEORGIA

Two grooms, one aisle
Join us as we wed in style
The pleasure of your company
is requested as
James Braxton Conway
and
Tyler Walter Garrison
tie the knot
Saturday, August 26, 2017
at four-thirty in the afternoon
Yardley's Yacht Club
525 Commercial Street
Provincetown, Massachusetts
Festive clambake and cocktails to follow

LESS FORMAL WEDDING INVITATIONS

While the rules of the social graces still apply to less formal wedding invitations, you can still be playful and casual—for instance, by mentioning the wedding website or promising dancing under the moonlight. Here are two examples:

Jane and Laura
are getting married!
Please come and share in their joy
on Sunday, April 15, 2018
at six o'clock
Stargazer Hotel
719 Canyon Road
Portland, Oregon
Dinner, dancing, and fireworks to follow

When You Don't Identify with a Gender

If you wish to honor your parents on the wedding invitation, you don't have to decide between using the term "son" or "daughter" when referring to yourself. Drop the gendered word and replace it with "child" or don't replace it at all. See the invitation example below.

MORI AND RACHEL LEVY
HAROLD AND HENRY GREEN-MATTHEWS
REQUEST THE HONOUR OF YOUR PRESENCE
AT THE MARRIAGE OF THEIR CHILDREN
ABIGAIL AND ELIZABETH
ON SATURDAY, THE NINTH OF DECEMBER
TWO THOUSAND EIGHTEEN
AT SIX O'CLOCK
CONGREGATION BEIT SIMCHAT TORAH
NEW YORK, NEW YORK

DIGITAL COMMUNICATION

Modern couples—especially the environmentally conscious—are turning more frequently to conveying wedding information electronically, from the save-the-date announcements to invitations and RSVPs and beyond.

PROS OF THE DIGITAL APPROACH

- Better for the environment
- Lower costs
- Less worry about items getting lost in the mail
- Ease of response for guests on devices they use daily
- Ability to update and download lists and information digitally

CONS OF THE DIGITAL APPROACH

- Leaves out older guests who don't use email or smart phones
- Potential for losing stored information due to uncontrollable glitches or apps and sites not working
- Lack of a personal touch
- Considered less formal by some people

THE MODERN WEDDING WEBSITE (AND APP!)

It's increasingly common for modern couples to create a wedding website (or "wedsite") during the wedding planning period. If you know enough HTML to handle selecting a theme and customizing it to your needs, you can make a great site using an out-of-the-box website page creator such as WordPress, Tumblr, SquareSpace, or Wix. But if you need more guidance, use a wedding website service such as The Knot, Wedding Paper Divas, Minted, Appy Couple, or Wedding Wire, which all have incredibly easy turnkey operations. Most websites are mobile-friendly now, but if you opt for a wedsite with a tech-forward company, such as Appy Couple, you'll also get a customized app for your wedding, allowing your guests to locate all your wedding info from the Appy Couple app on their smart phone. If budget is no issue and you'd like an even more customized web

The Art of the Guest List

GUEST EXPERT: AMBER HARRISON
wedding and etiquette expert, Wedding Paper Divas

One of the most exciting parts of wedding planning is dropping those beautiful, perfectly addressed invitations in the mail. Imagining the reactions of all your loved ones as they open their mailboxes and find your wedding invitation can make you giddy and full of anticipation. Unfortunately, getting to that moment can be difficult. Why? The guest list.

The guest list is a major point of negotiation (and often, sadly, conflict) for most couples and their families. Communication and compromise are key, but agreeing to a few ground rules before getting started might help you avoid some of the difficulty. Here are a few things to consider as you build your guest list:

Weddings at Work

Many of us spend so much time at the office that coworkers become great friends. Deciding which of your colleagues will make the cut can be a tough proposition. Where's the line? Here's a good rule of thumb: if you have friends at work you regularly spend time with outside of the office, go ahead and add them to your list.

While you are not obligated to invite colleagues to such a personal affair, be thoughtful of how your choices might impact your work environment. Will things feel awkward between you and your boss if you do not invite them? If you are concerned that excluding someone might cause trouble at the office, it's best to be generous and extend an extra invitation or two to ensure harmony.

Despite your overwhelming enthusiasm, it is very important that you curb your wedding-related conversations at work—especially if you are not planning to invite any or all of your colleagues.

Children

Clad in tiny tuxedos and perfectly delectable dresses, children can be a darling addition to any wedding. They are also unpredictable, which can be worrisome for some couples. Every couple must decide early on if they would like to include children in their wedding festivities. Keep in mind that it is okay to be selective about which children are invited. Just try to set a clear guideline, so that it isn't obvious to guests with unruly children that you intentionally excluded only their kids. For example, it would be appropriate to extend invitations only to the children in the wedding party and the children of immediate family members.

Clearly communicate which family members are invited by listing their names on the invitation. The omission of children's names signals that it is an adult-only affair. Sometimes, however, this subtle message goes unrecognized. To avoid potentially awkward situations, some couples choose to include the phrase "adults only" on their printed invitation. Personally, I suggest following the traditional invitation etiquette, followed up with a phone call in which you and the affected guests can have a gentle but honest conversation about your preference.

Once you've made a decision about kids at your wedding, stick with it. Exceptions will only cause questions and hurt feelings from other guests.

The Mandatory Guest

After you have both come up with a list of all the people you really want at your wedding, you will probably be left with a small handful of people who, for one reason or another, you feel obligated to invite. You know the type: an old friend you haven't kept in touch with, that one cousin who tends to cause a scene at every family gathering, the irritating partner of someone in your wedding party. You feel like you should invite them, but probably aren't too happy about the idea.

To help you decide, think about what will happen to your relationship if you don't invite this person. Who else does this decision affect? Will inviting the person put other friends or family members in an uncomfortable situation? Will not being invited make the person feel singled out or excluded—for example, if they're a distant cousin and the rest of the extended family is attending?

Weddings are emotional—for everyone! It is your day but remember that hurt feelings over a perceived slight can last a lifetime. The most important thing you can do in this situation is to embrace inclusiveness. When in doubt, find room for one more.

presence, hire a graphic designer and web developer to create the wedding website (and app!) of your dreams, one that can be turned into a family news site after you get married.

Include the following information on your wedding website:

- A welcome message
- Your names
- Where and when the wedding will be held, noting start times for the ceremony and the reception (especially if the reception doesn't immediately follow the ceremony)
- Hotel accommodations
- Transportation options
- Gift registries (kept toward the bottom of the page or at the end of the navigation menu so the focus remains on guests' presence at the wedding, not on the presents)
- Special instructions or suggestions on attire (such as black tie, or asking all the guests to wear white) or shoe choice (for instance, cautioning against wearing heels to an outdoor wedding on the grass)

Optional extras include:

- Your engagement story
- A hashtag for guests to use when they're at one of your wedding events
- Your Instagram and Twitter handles
- Additional events that everyone is invited to, such as a morning-after brunch
- An online RSVP option
- A fill-in-the-blank section for song requests
- Introductions to the wedding party

Tasks to Tackle

- Research stationery suites, styles, and themes.

- Hire a graphic artist to design a wedding logo or handle any artwork for your stationery. If the designer doesn't offer you a contractor's agreement or contract, write up the terms of your agreement yourself, including: delivery date for the work, a provision that the total cost will cover up to three revisions, and the stipulation that the art will be delivered in a high-resolution format that your printer can work with.

- Hire a photographer for engagement photos that can be used on your save-the-dates and/or your wedding website.

- Review all new contracts carefully. Feel free to negotiate revisions that are important to you, and ask for a final copy with all signatures.

- Order save-the-date announcements.

- Personally address your save-the-date announcements.

- Mail save-the-date announcements.

- Order invitations.

- Order personalized thank-you notes.

- Create a schedule for invitation pickup or delivery.

- Once invitations, etc., are received, begin hand-addressing the envelopes or deliver them to your calligrapher.

- Assemble completed invitations.

- Hand-stamp invitations.

- Mail invitations.

- Order or make the wedding programs.

- Order or make place cards.

- Order or make escort cards.

- Order or make the wedding menu.

CHAPTER SEVEN

HIRING WEDDING PROS

Whether your budget is robust or limited, one thing is clear when planning your wedding: you're going to require help orchestrating a full-scale event. But how do you assemble your dream team? Couples often feel overwhelmed at this stage, especially if they've never hired a DJ, planned a meal for more than a dozen people, or paired together a variety of flowers for color, scent, and meaning beyond what's available at the local grocery store.

Recommendations hold major weight at this stage of the game, whether they come from friends, websites, magazines, or other vendors. The creative professionals working for you will enable you to pull off what is likely to be one of the biggest parties of your life, as well as a meaningful ceremony in which you make one of the greatest commitments of your life. This chapter provides all you need to know when researching and employing them.

First and foremost, all your vendors should be equality-minded. No exceptions. You're not looking for someone to merely be tolerant for the sake of earning your money. What you deserve are professionals who personally believe in full marriage equality for every human being.

So how do you find such wonderful creative professionals? They're not unicorns, but they're more rare than you might think. Wedding vendors and venues, as a general rule, believe in love and bring a sense of purpose to their work of bringing your vision to life and helping you make this everlasting commitment in your relationship. Only a limited number of wedding professionals are interested in working with LGBTQ+ weddings, however, so it's important to know what they're doing to find you. Once you know how they operate, it'll be easier to find one of these equality-minded vendors.

Wedding vendors who want to reach LGBTQ+ couples typically:

- Advertise in LGBTQ+ wedding media outlets, such as equallywed.com
- Ask their current clientele to spread the word that they're equality-minded
- Use SEO and keywords such as "LGBTQ+ weddings," "gay weddings," "lesbian weddings," "same-sex weddings," and "marriage equality" on their websites to attract LGBTQ+ customers from search sites such as Google
- Feature LGBTQ+ weddings they've worked on in their online portfolio and/or in their marketing material
- Put up booths at local Pride festivals and wedding showcases for the LGBTQ+ market
- Coordinate with other wedding vendors on their interest in working with LGBTQ+ couples to build a reputation as an equality-minded vendor
- Contact media outlets to cover their weddings of LGBTQ+ couples, thereby receiving free advertising to help them reach potential new clients

A wedding vendor or venue you're considering may not have taken any of these steps, but that doesn't have to eliminate them from your list of possible hires. You'll just need to do more research to decide if the person or company is right for you. Obviously, an outright homophobic remark during the first conversation with a vendor will tell you immediately that they're not the one. But what about more subtle indications that they simply cannot handle the important responsibility of providing flawless, judgment-free service? In those situations, follow your gut instincts.

Camille and Adrienne's experience (next page) is a helpful case study outlining what could go wrong when you press on with a wedding vendor who doesn't know or doesn't care to learn how to best take care of you.

TESTING A VENDOR'S EQUALITY-MINDEDNESS

Vendors need to surpass all of your standards in order to win your business. You are paying them to help make your wedding day as perfect as possible. Follow these tips to make sure they're ready for your wedding:

1. **Research vendors**: Are they members of an equality organization such as the Human Rights Campaign, a state-level equality nonprofit, or the Wedding Equality Alliance? Are there badges on their website from *Equally Wed* signifying that they're an equality-minded wedding vendor? Do they feature real LGBTQ+ couples on their website? (Stock photos don't count.) Helpful clues like these suggest that a vendor is LGBTQ+-friendly.

2. **Ask questions**: Whether during your first call or email or after you've been in touch for a month, it's never a bad time to ask the vendor, "Have you ever worked with an LGBTQ+ wedding before?" If they have, ask them how it went. If they have not, ask them, "What are your thoughts on marriage equality?" or, "What are your thoughts on working with an LGBTQ+ couple?" Let the vendor answer. Be absolutely silent. The longer you wait to speak, the more they'll share. Most people want to fill the silence after a question, as well as give you more information, until it's absolutely clear that you're satisfied with the answer. While they're answering, be on the lookout for red-flag phrases (read: anything that makes you cringe). Offensive comments from seemingly kind

True Love Lessons

Camille and Adrienne experienced underhanded slights from their wedding planner, starting with their initial meeting, but politely overlooked them. Here's their experience in Camille's words:

I was elated when Adrienne asked me to marry her on a park bench near the Eiffel Tower. It was day two of our vacation, and her romantic proposal at the beginning of our trip gave our entire adventure more energy and excitement, as we couldn't stop gushing to ourselves and to complete strangers that we were engaged! As soon as we returned to the States, I expected a similar reception. I was flying on cloud nine and wasn't expecting any issues from those close to Adrienne and myself, nor really from anyone else. After all, we live in Massachusetts, the first state to offer marriage equality. Who wouldn't be happy for two women in love and deciding to commit the rest of their lives to each other? The answer was surprising.

We found Emily, our wedding planner, online from a wedding resource website that had a gay section—a specific area of the vendor directory that vendors are in when they want to work with same-sex couples. At least, that's how we understood it.

Emily did a fabulous job with many facets of our wedding, but she made comments that really bothered us that we didn't quite know how to handle. When we discussed flowers, she cracked jokes about who would carry the bouquet. We both planned to, but she seemed to be mocking us for it.

We don't think we were being sensitive by being offended by her off-color jokes throughout the process. She kept making comments that implied that what we wanted was somehow abnormal from what she typically does. But we didn't know what we could do so far in—and she had secured a hefty 50% deposit. We decided to stick it out. Our wedding ended up being amazing, but our experience with our wedding planner's ignorance soured a good portion of our planning experience.

If we have any advice to give, it's this: triple-check your vendors right away for their gay friendliness and familiarity with LGBTQ+ couples and weddings. It matters more than we knew.

people can irk you longer than you might imagine, and leave you wondering if they value your relationship with your partner as much as a heterosexual couple's relationship.

3. **Talk with other vendors**: Ask vendors you're already comfortable with for their recommendations for wedding pros in the areas you still need to hire. Chances are, they'll recommend some mighty fine people you'll love because vendors tend to recommend only creatives they enjoy working with and who'll make them look good too.

WEDDING PLANNERS

You don't have to have a wedding planner—it's a luxury. And with the right choice of wedding vendors and extra effort on your own part, you can easily get by without one. But if your budget allows, it can be well worth the investment to hire the right wedding planner for your needs.

The great wedding planners do much more than help you negotiate contracts and choose between the blush- and bashful-colored seat covers. They're part counselor, part business adviser, part florist, part designer, part dreamer, part bulldog, and all kinds of creative. Besides ensuring that you're receiving high-quality treatment from other vendors, they review contracts, negotiate on your behalf, and make sure you're asking the right questions. You want a well-connected planner who's committed to working within your budget *and* who respects those elements of the wedding that are most important to you. Your planner should be able to recommend quality vendors at several price points.

Full-service wedding planners completely immerse themselves in your vision, and indeed, this is as it should be. Their ideas matter, but they should listen to you, honoring and respecting your wishes. And if you haven't got a clue as to how you want your wedding to look, a good wedding planner will ask the right questions to guide you toward realizing your own vision.

What a wedding planner shouldn't do is minimize your choices or question the validity of your partnership. You should feel entirely comfortable with your wedding planner and how they orchestrate all parts of your big day and the moments around it. After all, this is the vendor you're going to be spending the most time with. It's important for you to get along—and to have it your way (within reason).

QUESTIONS TO ASK WHEN HIRING A WEDDING PLANNER

- How long have you been in business? *If the planner is new to this line of work, they probably will not have built up relationships with other vendors and may lack the negotiating experience you're going to need.*

- Have you ever worked with an LGBTQ+ couple before? *Familiarity with the LGBTQ+ community and history is critical for someone you'll be working with so closely.*

- What's your idea of a perfect wedding? *An ideal wedding planner wants to make the couple as happy as possible, not impose their own ideas but rather make suggestions based on research and experience.*

- What's your plan if you are sick the day of my wedding? *If an unavoidable emergency occurs in your wedding planner's life on your wedding day, they should have a backup planner lined up who will be armed with your day-of itinerary and comprehensive documentation on everything anyone needs to know who's working on your wedding.*

- Who are some of your favorite wedding vendors and venues in the area where I'm getting married? *A good wedding vendor knows nearly everyone worth knowing in the wedding industry in your region.*

- What type of role do you play on the day of the wedding? *If you want someone attending to every detail, following your itinerary, and making sure every other vendor is in line with your vision, make your wishes known to your planner or coordinator. Better yet, get it in writing so there are no assumptions.*

Tasks to Tackle

- Vet your vendors.

- Evaluate each vendor's and venue's equality-mindedness.

- Review each and every contract carefully before you sign it. Are you okay with the terms? Feel free to ask for revisions. Make sure everything verbally agreed upon is in the contract before you sign it or else you'll have no legal recourse if things go sour. Make sure you get a final copy of the contract with both parties' signatures.

- Keep track of every hired vendor's contact information, estimated cost, actual cost, payment due date, and when you've paid in full.

- Decide if you want to hire a wedding planner.

CHAPTER EIGHT

PHOTOGRAPHY AND VIDEOGRAPHY

Choosing the person or team who will provide photos and videos of your wedding is a critical decision. In capturing your wedding, photography and videography cement your day in history. As you gaze upon your wedding photos for years to come and sit down to watch your wedding video, the memories will come flooding back to you of one of the biggest and most important days of your lives. If you have children or plan to, these mementos also serve as time capsules. Naturally, such an important task shouldn't be entrusted to just anyone. You probably won't get a redo of your wedding, so it's important to select a professional who knows what they're doing, whose work you like, and who doesn't have another task to attend to at your wedding (like being a guest).

HIRING A WEDDING PHOTOGRAPHER

Your choice of wedding photographer matters not just because of the images they will produce but also because you'll be physically closer to them than to any of your other vendors. This creative professional will be somewhat intimate with you and your partner: zooming in with a mega-lens while you kiss, guiding you into romantic embraces for photo ops, and then witnessing your love over and over as they edit the images. You want the photographer to feel comfortable around you just as much as the photographer needs to make you feel at ease. A symbiotic relationship between the couple and the photographer(s) enables everyone to breathe and just be who they are. If you're not an actor or model, chances are you've never been formally photographed mid-smooch, but being comfortable and relaxed with the photographer can translate into you looking your best in your engagement and wedding photos.

There are a few elements to keep in mind as you consider possible photographers.

LGBTQ+ EXPERIENCE • Without exception, the most important consideration is to hire only vendors who are wholly supportive of your relationship. This is especially essential with your photographers, who are going to be all up in your romantic business. But more than just being supportive, it's even better if they have experience working with LGBTQ+ couples in some capacity. Here's why: Some photographers have built their entire career on pigeonholing their couples into gender-specific, heterosexual ideals of what's the "norm." These types of shutterbugs tend to try to create images of a strong, strapping man protecting the feminine princess bride. Though sometimes we do see this dynamic in LGBTQ+ relationships (and that's great too), it's not okay for a photographer to push you to conform to a role that doesn't suit you. In fact, this goes for straight couples too and not just LGBTQ+ couples.

Look for wedding photographers who have already worked with LGBTQ+ couples and who showcase them on their website along with everyone else, rather than segregate them in another category all their own. Don't be shy about asking potential photographers if they have experience with LGBTQ+ couples if you don't see any mention of it on their website or in their marketing materials. It's a rough lesson to learn after you have hired someone who takes exceptional photos but is putting you and your partner into over-the-top heteronormative poses because they don't know how to do otherwise.

PHOTOGRAPHY AESTHETICS • There's a wide variety of photography and videography aesthetics, so during your search for the right documentarian of your wedding, carefully study the visual styles of these professionals to find one that best articulates your vision. As you explore wedding photographers' online portfolios of work, either on their own websites or through photo-sharing apps such as Instagram, you'll notice that each has their own style. The trend in modern wedding photography is photojournalism, which aims to tell the narrative of your love story through candid photos—though some of them are styled. Traditional wedding photographers are the most likely to ask everyone to smile for the camera and are focused on the classic moments of the wedding, from the processional to the cutting of the cake.

You'll also find some commercial photographers who shoot weddings on the side. They're quite talented at taking still photos and styling your wedding shoes and rings, capturing them at just the right angle and light, yet they may be less adept at photographing moving subjects. Couples usually want a blend of all three of these types of photographers and can find it by researching portfolios thoroughly to discover a wedding photographer who is artistic and talented and can also make your granny happy with some posed family shots too.

CHEMISTRY: MEETING WITH YOUR PHOTOGRAPHER • The next important consideration to keep in mind as you seek the right photographer is your chemistry with this person. If your photographer makes you uncomfortable, your photos won't be authentic.

Once you've narrowed your search to your favorites, arrange a meeting with each of the photographers you have in mind. Ask them to show you their portfolio. (Ask in advance so they'll be sure to bring it.) You're looking for not just their online highlight reel, but for a full wedding album so you can see the range they're capable of. Have special effects and photo editing been used on only a few images? Is the aesthetic consistent throughout? How are the couples positioned in their portraits? Is this how you'd like to be positioned, or does the pose look like it would feel awkward and dated? It is of paramount importance that your wedding photos be as you like them, so if you're not feeling a potential photographer's vibe—whether it's their work or their demeanor—move on.

When you find someone you truly enjoy, take the time to discuss pertinent details to avoid unexpected surprises later.

QUESTIONS TO ASK WHEN HIRING A PHOTOGRAPHER

- Have you ever shot an LGBTQ+ couple's wedding before? *Ask to view the photographer's portfolio of a previous LGBTQ+ wedding and also ask for references so you can interview the couple. Ask them whether their wedding was a recent one, and how the photographer behaved at the wedding.*

- How do you feel about marriage equality? *The answer should convey complete and utter comfort with LGBTQ+ people. If the photographer hesitates at all, or makes jokes in bad taste, this isn't an equality-minded wedding photographer.*

- We want to be treated equally—neither of us in this couple is more important than the other. We may have two groups of wedding attendants, we may have two mother-son dances, two father-daughter dances, or another variation, and we may have two getting-ready suites. Will you be able to keep all that in mind when shooting?

- Do you shoot film or digital? *Each produces its own aesthetic, so if you've got a liking for one or the other, make sure to do your research here, as film photographers are making a big comeback, especially among the luxury set.*
- What's your photography style?
- How do you feel about couple and family portraits?
- Do you prefer black-and-white or color photos? *A digital photographer shoots in color and then converts to black-and-white for dramatic effect or to fix strange colors. If you don't discuss this issue up front, you may end up with more black-and-white photos or more color photos than you bargained for.*
- Do you have a second shooter? *A photography assistant can capture other angles of important moments. Ask to see samples of their work too, as well as confirm their support of marriage equality.*
- What's your availability on my wedding day? *Make sure the photographer can commit to the entire time you want them for, which might include the period getting ready before the wedding or the after-party.*
- Are you available to shoot the rehearsal dinner or the morning-after brunch?
- What's the rate for extra time?
- If you're shooting with film, will we be charged for the rolls?
- How many edited photos can we expect to get from the wedding day?
- How will our guests view and order the photos?
- How will you deliver the proofs?
- Will I get the high-resolution watermark-free photos in a digital file, by either email or thumb drive?
- Is there a minimum order for prints?
- Do you bring your own lighting? *The answer should be yes. Ideally you want someone who uses unobtrusive equipment.*
- Have you worked at our venue before? If not, will you visit it in advance?

What's Up with Copyrights?

Pro photographers Shana Perry and Brittney Love, married couple and owners of Massachusetts-based Love & Perry Photography and Films, explain that the copyright to wedding photos is protected by the federal copyright law and will always belong to the photographer unless it is legally transferred to the client via a written contract. "This is very rare, that any photographer would give over the copyright to the photos," say Shana and Brittney. "It would be like a painter selling their painting to someone and allowing them to claim it as their own, reproduce it, and sell the images. So when clients choose a package that includes all of the digital and download rights to their photos, we give them an image usage/print release agreement in their contract. This allows them to download, print, and share the images for personal use only. No commercial use will be given unless they have our permission in writing and blood (insert evil, villainous laugh here)."

- What's your backup plan if you're sick on my wedding day?
- What's your plan if your equipment fails on the day of my wedding?
- If you are part of a photography team or company, how can I ensure that you're the one who will show up on my wedding day?
- What is your cancellation policy?
- What's your turnaround time on wedding photos? *Make sure the turnaround time is in the contract. Some couples mistakenly believe they'll receive photos right after the wedding, only to be kept waiting for a year.*
- Do you charge extra for travel? *For booking ease, some photographers now include their travel expenses inside their packages.*
- When are payments due?
- Are you willing to work off a shot list? *Most photographers are familiar with this concept—a shot list is a directive detailing the photos you want to make sure you get.*

- What do you wear for weddings? *If you have a preference on color and attire, speak now or forever hold your peace. Your photographer needs to be comfortable, but you can ask them to wear all black, including black sneakers, to blend in.*
- What are the usage guidelines for our wedding photos? Will we be able to share the photos at our leisure? *You're looking for unrestricted personal use only, such as being able to submit the photos to blogs, with photography credit and permission, as well as display them on your social media channels and in your home. See the sidebar for more on usage.*

HIRING A VIDEOGRAPHER

Having a videographer at your wedding—especially one with artistic talent and professional editing skills—is like starring in a romantic movie, with you and your sweetheart as the lead actors. It's a gorgeous way to relive certain moments from your wedding day by watching yourselves and your loved ones in clips worthy of the silver screen. Videography is labor-intensive—in both the shooting and the editing—and just as with photography, you get what you pay for. If you want a true cinematic masterpiece that captures your wedding, spring for the best you can afford and search for wedding cinematographers.

After finding a videographer whose style wows you both visually and auditorially, meet up to discuss critical components of their work—and make sure you jibe. The videographer will sometimes be even closer to you than a photographer, so it's imperative that you feel comfortable with them.

QUESTIONS TO ASK WHEN HIRING A VIDEOGRAPHER
- What's your experience with LGBTQ+ weddings?
- How long have you been doing weddings? How many have you been the lead videographer on?
- Will there be a second shooter, a stationary camera, or any other backup cameras on hand for our wedding? *Without a second shooter or other backup, it may be difficult or nearly impossible for your videographer to capture every moment. A second shooter often comes*

with the videography package, but it's important to ask now instead of making assumptions.

- Are there any other pros in the area you love to work with? *Wedding videographers should be pretty well connected. If they've worked well with another local pro, such as a photographer, you may want to hire that person too.*

- How would you describe your style? Is it more documentary, cinematic, or a mix? *Even if you've watched one or two of their videos on their website, it's important to make sure the videographer's style aligns with yours. If you want a romantic video but you and your videographer don't have the same idea of what that means, you could end up paying for a video you don't really want. Also, ask for sample videos to get a sense of the videographer's talent and professionalism.*

- How does your pricing work? *Videographers typically charge a flat rate based on time. Some offer preset packages that include other elements, such as a same-day edit or an extra shooter. Even if you're buying just the standard package, it's important to go over what's included. And if there's something you want that's not covered in the contract—be it a short snippet to share with family or a hard drive with all of the raw footage— bring this up before hiring the videographer and make sure it's included in the written agreement.*

- Have you ever worked with my photographer? Do you know my

Photo Trends

Drone photography and videography is on the rise. Drones capture stunning aerial views and 360-degree images of important moments. Be sure that your drone operator is licensed and insured (drones can be dangerous), and be sure to view their work ahead of time to confirm that their experience is worth the additional cost.

photographer? *The photographer and videographer will need to work closely together throughout your event to capture all of your moments in the best way possible without blocking each other's angles. If they've worked together before, they'll most likely work well again. If they've never worked together before, that's fine, but it's important that they meet beforehand to talk about the format and how they'll get it all shot.*

- What kind of lighting equipment do you have? *Look for a videographer who uses modern video cameras with built-in lighting capabilities.*
- What's your strategy for capturing sound? *Being able to hear the vows as well as the toasts and other important verse is essential to a good video. The right videographer knows how to discreetly plant microphones in flowers or on the couple's attire.*
- Will we be able to see a rough version before you edit?
- Have you worked at our venue before? If not, will you visit it in advance?
- What's your backup plan if you're sick on my wedding day?
- If you are part of a videography team or company, how can I ensure that you're the one who will show up on my wedding day?
- What is your cancellation policy?
- When are payments due?
- What do you wear for weddings? *As when you're interviewing photographers, if you have preferences on attire, do speak up now. Your*

videographer also needs to be comfortable, but can also be asked to blend in by wearing all black.

- Can we speak with some of your recent couples?
- How long will the final cut be?
- How long does it take you to produce the final video?
- Will we be able to have a say in the editing process, including the background music?
- What type of video format will you provide at the end? Can we share it online?
- What are the usage guidelines for our wedding video? Will we be able to share the video at our leisure?

Tasks to Tackle

- Research photo and video styles that appeal to you.
- Schedule your engagement photo session six to eight months prior to the wedding, especially if you'll be using these photos on your save-the-date announcements and wedding website.
- Meet with your photographer and videographer to go over every detail.
- Put down a deposit for your photographer and videographer.
- Review each and every contract carefully before you sign. Are you okay with the terms? Feel free to ask for revisions. Make sure everything verbally agreed upon appears in the written document before you sign it to ensure you'll have legal recourse if things go sour. Get a final copy of the contract with both parties' signatures.
- A month or two before the wedding, revisit your agreements with your photographer and videographer, go over the shot list, and inform them of any special family traditions or strained relationships.
- Meet again with your photographer and videographer about a month before the wedding to go over shot lists, timing, and the schedule of the day.

CHAPTER NINE

WELCOMING YOUR GUESTS

Weddings are an incredibly special time when everyone you love and care about can gather in your honor. Your guests are spending money and giving up time to be available for you and this momentous occasion in your life. It's only kind, then, to make their experience as comfortable and enjoyable as possible. You can do this by setting up lodging options for them—and at various price points—assessing their transportation needs, and welcoming them with gift bags.

GUEST ACCOMMODATIONS

No matter whether you're marrying in your hometown or having a destination wedding, it's standard to select at least two lodging options for your wedding guests that are close to the wedding venue—one on the higher end and one that's more budget-friendly. Call each hotel you are suggesting to your guests and ask for a certain number of rooms to be reserved in your event name (e.g., "the Green-White wedding"). This is called a room block and ensures (up to a certain deadline) that your guests can get a reservation even if there are other significant events simultaneously taking place on or around your wedding date. Don't guarantee the rooms to the hotel unless you want to pay for them if there are leftover rooms. Be sure to share the lodging information on your wedding website. For extra ease, link to the hotel's website.

GUEST TRANSPORTATION

Being responsible for transporting your wedding guests between the main hotel and the wedding venue has become commonplace—that is, the nearlyweds usually cover this cost. If you're willing and able to take on this responsibility, talk to your hotel about transportation options, such as a hotel van or shuttle, and also look into renting a chartered bus, a city trolley, or several stretch limos. You could even have a line of prepaid (including gratuity) cars waiting for guests at scheduled times.

GUEST WELCOME BAGS

One of the best ways to kick off the wedding weekend is by placing welcome bags in all of the guests' rooms, whether they're staying in one or two hotels for a hometown wedding or at a resort for a destination wedding (where welcome bags have become very common and easy to do). Welcome bags run the gamut from linen bags imprinted or embroidered with the couple's monogram or names or a romantic quote, to woven baskets, to standard gift bags purchased at your local grocer. Hotels are familiar with this tradition and will deliver the bags to the rooms for you.

A welcome bag might include:

- A map of the city
- A souvenir from the city
- A wedding itinerary of events, with addresses and start times (include only events that everyone is invited to)
- A welcome note from the couple
- One bottle of water per room guest

- Phone numbers for honor attendants and parents or other elders to answer their questions (signaling to guests that people other than the couple are available to help them in any way)
- Popular sightseeing options or activities if the weekend will include significant downtime
- Small snacks, such as nuts or granola bars or a confection from a local baker
- Wedding hashtags for social media

Tasks to Tackle

- ▦ Choose hotels for guests.
- ▦ Request room blocks.
- ▦ Plan out transportation for guests.
- ▦ Assemble welcome bags.

CHAPTER TEN

PLANNING THE CEREMONY

Perhaps the most important element of your wedding is the reason everyone has gathered: the moment you and your beloved vow to love and cherish each other forever. Choosing among both time-honored traditions and modern rituals to make your wedding ceremony your own is an incredibly personal decision. One way to begin is to select the person who will be essential to your wedding: the ceremony officiant, the overseer of your covenant of marriage.

SELECTING AN OFFICIANT

The person you and your beloved will need the most for your wedding ceremony is the officiant. Because this person is so vital to your day, you'll want to get them booked well before any other vendor.

Choosing an officiant should start with deciding what type of ceremony you're interested in having. Will it be spiritual, religious, or secular? If you want a religious ceremony, your officiant choice might already be made for you if you're a member of a congregation. Of course, even if you are a member, you still might not be allowed to have your wedding at your house of worship. (For more on this, visit Chapter 5 on venues.)

QUESTIONS TO ASK WHEN CHOOSING AN OFFICIANT

- Have you worked with LGBTQ+ couples before?
- What are your travel fees?
- How do you feel about incorporating more than one religion, ritual, or cultural style into the ceremony? *Some religious leaders will be restricted from making changes, so it's best to ask early what can and cannot happen—for instance, would you be able to incorporate the Jewish tradition of breaking glass into a Catholic church wedding?*
- Can you share sample ceremony texts and ritual concepts to give us an idea of your creative vision?
- Where can we see videos of you performing ceremonies to get a feel for your speaking style?
- Will you share contact information with one or two of your past couples whom we could contact for referrals?

Perhaps your chosen officiant is someone you've known forever—a priest, rabbi, or minister from your childhood, for example, or the clergyperson at your current house of worship. Your officiant could be a close friend, ordained for your marriage only, or a judge or justice of the peace.

It's important to make sure that whoever is solemnizing your marriage is available for your wedding date and time. In fact, their availability might dictate when your wedding will be held, so find out their availability before booking venues and other vendors.

Even if you've known your chosen officiant for a long time, they'll want to become more familiar with you as a couple, as well as glean your vision for the ceremony and your thoughts on marriage. Take care to discuss these critical elements with your officiant:

- Date and time of wedding ceremony
- Date and time of wedding rehearsal (typically held the day before; be sure to reserve the venue for the wedding rehearsal)
- How long the rehearsal will run (so you can plan for the rehearsal dinner)

- Whether there are fees for the rehearsal
- Your ideas and the officiant's ideas for personalizing the ceremony—in order to make sure all are on the same page, you're comfortable with the officiant's suggestions, and the officiant is willing to make your requested changes
- Religious beliefs that will dictate some or all of the ceremony
- The flow of the parts of the ceremony
- How you'll be pronounced as married ("wife and wife," "spouses forever," "lawfully wedded husbands," "partners in life," etc.)
- The length of the ceremony
- The officiant's fee or donation request
- The names you want the officiant to use in the ceremony (your nicknames or special pronunciations), as well as whether either of you is changing your name
- What you want your officiant to wear
- Arrangements for premarital counseling if required by your religion or otherwise desired (the benefits are numerous!)

A SAMPLE WEDDING CEREMONY SCHEDULE

- Prelude music plays.
- Honored guests are ushered to their seats.
- The processional music begins.
- The wedding party enters one by one or two by two.
- Different music plays for the couple entering, whether one by one, together, or accompanied by a loved one.
- The officiant opens with a greeting.
- The couple declare their wish to marry and exchange vows and rings.
- The officiant proclaims the couple married.
- The couple kisses.
- The recessional music begins.
- The couple recesses first, followed by the wedding party.

Three Tips for Planning a Meaningful Ceremony

GUEST EXPERT: BETHEL NATHAN
ordained officiant open to all
Ceremonies by Bethel, San Diego, California

The ceremony is the core of the wedding. It transforms a party into a wedding. Here's how to make it meaningful:

First, find the right person to speak for you and be your voice on this day and to walk you through the process. I think that finding the officiant who fits you, supports you and your connection, and will help you get the ceremony that is you is crucial. You want the words spoken that day to reflect your relationship and how you see love and commitment. Having a genuine and authentic ceremony, whatever that is for you, will make a difference not only in your celebration but in how all of your guests see you two from here on out.

Second, be prepared to devote time to creating a ceremony that fits you, whether that involves writing your own vows, choosing readings (which can be not only poetry or interesting pieces but also song lyrics or quotes), or finding rituals that speak to you. Many officiants will walk you through this; if you're considering an officiant who does not, definitely ask up front about how much flexibility you have in creating your ceremony. My couples complete two written assignments for me, filling out incredibly detailed questionnaires so that I can learn their history, how they see each other and what they share, and what is important to them. Their input enables me to create a personal and meaningful ceremony. Even if others have expectations about what your ceremony should contain (or should not contain), remember that it needs to fit you two first and foremost.

And lastly, enjoy the process. Your ceremony—and the process you go through to create it—should inspire not only your family and friends but you two as well. It should remind you of where you've been together, what your present feels like, and what you look forward to in your future. You two are forever, and that is what should matter the most of all.

APPROACHING THE AISLE

Deciding who will process down the aisle, and when and with whom, keeps some couples up at night, but let your own heart guide you. Your options are wide open: you can walk up the aisle together, one of you can walk in from the side with the officiant, you can walk up the aisle separately, you can walk up two different aisles separately at the same time, you can walk up separately with escorts, or you can do something else entirely—such as walk up with a marching band or your wedding party. You could even descend on the crowd via aerial ropes. To thine own heart be true!

EMBRACING TRADITIONS

Many LGBTQ+ weddings claim the traditions from heterosexual weddings that fit our needs and discard those that do not serve us or honor our relationships. Our marriages are equal in value and meaning to those of cisgender heterosexuals, yet our ceremonies may have two people of opposite genders, one or more people who are transgender, one or more people who are neutral in their gender, or one or more people who identify with two (or more) genders. These possibilities alone make our weddings different from what society deems typical.

But the significance of our ability to legally wed goes much deeper than this. Our fight for marriage recognition has been arduous. The work that our community did to achieve it makes our weddings all the more meaningful now, which is why LGBTQ+ couples often look to our history for inspiration and meaning to bring to our ceremonies.

Historically, we have not been able to have our weddings legally recognized in the United States, and other countries and colonies continue to battle over one of the most contentious social issues of our time. Until states began legally recognizing same-sex marriage—Massachusetts was the first in 2004 in *Goodridge v. Department of Public Health*—many same-sex couples committing themselves to each other did so in what was usually called a "commitment ceremony." From 2004 until 2015, couples seeking legal recognition of their marriage flocked to the states that offered marriage equality. They had either destination weddings in those states or civil unions at a city hall before traveling home for a wedding.

When someone in the LGBTQ+ community marries, it's an opportunity to proudly proclaim our right to have a partner in life, to be in love, to be loved, and to marry. Because LGBTQ+ marriage and commitment ceremonies often took place in secret before the public began slowly accepting LGBTQ+ couples and their relationships, pride is an incredibly significant element of LGBTQ+ weddings.

PERSONALIZING YOUR CEREMONY WITH CULTURE AND MEANING

Whether you're a practicing religious couple or not will dictate some of the elements of your wedding ceremony. But even in a religious ceremony, there are an incredible number of options when planning how your ceremony may vary from the typical schedule (see page 88). Whether it's hand fasting, readings, ring warming, chocolate feeding, unity candles, sand pouring, or canvas painting—just several of the many options—some of the following examples may inspire you and your spouse-to-be.

THE MARRIAGE COVENANT OR KETUBAH • In the Jewish faith, couples have a written agreement that is a nonlegal marriage contract; this document covers many issues for the most devout Jewish people. Historically, ketubahs explained the dowry that the bride's father was offering, shared information such as if the bride was a virgin, and ensured that the husband could not strip the wife of material possessions she was entitled to. The traditional ketubah is signed by the rabbi and two witnesses who aren't related to the couple.

Before marriage equality, the idea of the ketubah was picked up by non-Jewish LGBTQ+ couples who didn't have the legal marriage certificate to sign to go along with their wedding. It remains popular in the United States, as well as in other countries where citizens are still fighting for marriage equality. In Jewish and non-Jewish LGBTQ+ couples' weddings, modern ketubahs are a written testament to the couple's commitment to each other. Some couples hire artists to design elaborate ketubahs for their marriage. Though the couple isn't required to sign them, many modern celebrants want to, along with their officiant and witnesses (usually honor attendants, but parents or other loved ones can sign as well). Then they can hang it in their home as a loving reminder of their commitment to each other.

HAND FASTING • A hand fasting—wrapping the couple's hands together with ribbon, fabric, or cord—is a pagan wedding ceremony believed to date back to sixteenth-century Celtic Scotland. Many pagans, Wiccans, nonbelievers, and faith-filled couples now use this marriage rite. To bind yourself in marriage via hand fasting is to literally tie the knot, so it's no wonder the ritual is making a comeback. The feeling of being bound to your beloved with ribbons or cords in an ancient ritual is magical and may appeal most to those having an outdoor wedding.

There are plenty of ways to adapt this tradition to your own wedding. First, go with your spouse-to-be to a fabric store, where each of you will select at least three ribbons of different colors that have special meaning for you. Look for hues that honor your heritage or the month of your birth or that have some other significance. Two to three feet of ribbon in each color is sufficient. Before the wedding, braid your ribbons together and have your spouse-to-be braid theirs. Then you can either braid your ribbons together into one cord or leave them separate until the ceremony.

The hand fasting can happen before, during, or after the vows have been said. When it's time, you will join hands, and your officiant will tuck one end of the ribbons into one of your palms (you'll discreetly hold it there with your thumb) and then begin wrapping the ribbons around both of your hands while speaking about your commitment to each other. Some couples have preselected members of the audience to come up and wrap ribbons of their own around the couple's hands as well, which can make for an especially communal feeling.

PERSONALIZED MUSIC • If one or both of you is musically inclined, consider singing or playing a special song. Or think about surprising your betrothed with your own performance. Consider asking a loved one to perform a musical piece you've selected if they're experienced in playing for a crowd. Nothing wows a crowd more than a heartfelt dedicated piece of music.

LIGHTING A CANDLE • The lighting of the unity candle is a widely practiced ritual at ceremonies. Although especially common in Protestant churches, anyone can do it—just double-check with your venue to make sure that candles are okay. When family is involved, a candle lighting can be even more moving.

To get it started, have two parents or other significant elders in your lives each light a slim tapered candle at the beginning of the ceremony. They will place their lit candles in candleholders on either side of the main candle, which is preferably a pillar shape. After you and your spouse have exchanged vows and rings, you'll each take the candle that your significant elder lit and together light the main candle. Then you have two options: extinguishing the tapered candles, which symbolizes the strength of the family coming together, or letting the tapered candles continue to burn, which symbolizes the strength of independent minds joining together equally but also celebrates individuality. Opening the candle lighting to children from a previous marriage or your new one can be especially heartwarming. The kids will receive their own tapered candles and can come in when you and your spouse do, just before, or right after.

HONORING THOSE WHO HAVE DIED

Weddings can be emotionally challenging for people who have lost loved ones, especially if the loss is recent. Even adults who lost parents when they were children may find themselves feeling the loss all over again because of the societal expectation that their parents

TANGIE AND MELISSA YOUNG-HOOKS

Melissa and I live our lives honoring, remembering, and keeping our loved ones who have passed away sacred. Although they are no longer with us, we felt it was only natural to have them present. The items we included on our ancestors table were: pictures, candles, water, money, a box of crystals, handmade music notes, roses, and a table runner made by my grandmother. We honored both recent family members who have passed away as well as those who passed away long ago, even before we were born. The ancestors table was located underneath a gazebo near our ceremony space and where the cocktail hour was. When they were ready, our guests stepped into the gazebo to hold the space of passed loved ones. We placed signage on the table, which read: "Those that we love / the ones that have passed away / walk beside us every day / as we continue to live / they live through us."

should have been there for the magical day. Those feelings of sadness and grief might make you feel guilty to be having a celebration at all. But there are a number of ways in which you can honor your deceased loved ones and, by doing so, feel like you have them at your wedding.

You can leave an empty guest chair with the name of your deceased loved one on it, adding the boutonniere or wrist corsage they might have worn. You can have your officiant mention your loved one by name during the ceremony, or if it's important to you to remember more than one deceased relative, the officiant can make a statement about all the loved ones who are no longer living.

RING WARMING

Having your rings warmed—or blessed—by some or all of your wedding guests is a nice way to call attention to one of the purposes of a wedding guest: to commit themselves to helping you in your marriage and to bear witness to the commitment you are making. Typically, an honor attendant will place both wedding rings in a small pouch and hand this to the officiant when asked. Then the officiant will announce the beginning of the ring warming. If it's a small wedding, all guests will be asked to warm the rings in their hands. If you have more than twenty guests, it's more practical to have only the first few rows of guests warm the rings, with each quietly making a wish of happiness for the couple or saying a prayer for the marriage. Once the rings have been warmed, an honor attendant collects them and returns them to the officiant or holds on to them until it is time for the ring exchange.

CHOCOLATE CEREMONIES

The purpose of the chocolate ceremony is to act out the sweetness, nuttiness, spiciness, and bitterness of life and the couple's willingness to take it all as it comes—together. Life, like a box of chocolates, is an adventure full of surprises that you're embarking on together. Chocolate favors round out this fun ritual, led by the officiant. Here is a sample script:

> Today, _____ and _____ will feed each other small amounts of chocolate to represent how they plan to navigate and appreciate their marriage. Chocolate, in any of its forms, nourishes our bodies and our souls. For _____ and _____, chocolate is a special treat that they indulge in to bring them joy or nourish their souls. Today, _____ and _____ recognize that their marriage also is a sweet treat that will bring joy to their lives and nourish their souls.

SAND POURING

A recurring theme at weddings is the joining together of families, whether families of origin or families of choice. In the ritual of sand pouring, each nearlywed has a vase of colored sand that they pour into a new vase together to symbolize their marriage and how, together, they are that much more beautiful. If families with children are being blended by this marriage, it can be particularly expressive for the children to pour their own special colored sand into the vase at the same time, signifying their support of the union and their choice to join this family.

With Me in Spirit

MY FATHER DIED JUST BEFORE MY WEDDING

My dad was my biggest cheerleader and believed wholeheartedly in equality. He celebrated my coming out from the moment I told him, frequently brought me gay and lesbian newspapers, and got to know anyone I dated. When Maria proposed, he was the first one I called. He was over the moon and couldn't wait to walk me down the aisle. I longed for my father-daughter dance. But it never came. My father died of sudden cardiac arrest just eight months before the wedding. It was devastating. I felt like my chest had been kicked in, and I didn't know how to go on with the wedding planning.

I took time to grieve, to sob, to mourn. But ultimately I decided to go forward with my wedding plans on the date we had already chosen because it was about officially joining my heart to a person whom my father believed I should be with. My father adored Maria.

On our wedding day, my florist sewed a beautiful pink rectangular pillow made from her grandmother's silk. She glued dusty miller leaves on it, which I also had in my bouquet. Then she pinned my father's freesia boutonniere to the pillow and placed it in the seat he would have taken after hugging me at the altar. My father's older brother—his only sibling—did a reading at my wedding about how we could feel my father's presence in earthly elements. When he read a line about feeling my dad in the blowing of the wind, we all felt a gentle breeze float through on what was otherwise a stifling June evening in our garden ceremony.

CANVAS PAINTING

A relatively new trend is couples painting a canvas together at the wedding ceremony. A canvas, easel, brushes, and paint are all set up on a table near the altar or chuppah long before the ceremony (but not so long that the paint starts to dry up). Just before or after the vows and rings are exchanged, the officiant directs the couple to the canvas and asks them to make strokes in different colors to show the blending of their creativity and the joining of their hearts. After the ceremony, guests can be invited to paint their own small swishes and shapes. The result is a wonderful keepsake for the couple's home.

BREAKING GLASS

Glass breaking is a tradition taken from heterosexual Jewish weddings: the groom smashes his foot onto a glass vessel to symbolize the destruction of the Temple in Jerusalem in A.D. 70. Nowadays many Jewish couples break the glass together—and some non-Jewish couples, including LGBTQ+ couples, are incorporating the tradition into their ceremonies as well.

The breaking of the glass not only symbolizes the terror that Jewish people faced but also reminds everyone in attendance that there is unhappiness and unrest in the world but they are incredibly blessed to experience the happiness and safety at the wedding. Because of the tragedies that have befallen the LGBTQ+ community, this ritual performed at LBGTQ+ weddings also now symbolizes the lives lost. Incidentally, in Italian weddings the glass is broken at the reception. The number of shards is said to indicate the number of happy years the couple will have together.

JUMPING THE BROOM

Broom jumping is believed to have originated in Ghana, Africa. Africans from this region who were kidnapped and taken to America to be sold as slaves continued this tradition in their marriage ceremonies, which were not legally recognized. Many African and African-American couples still include this tradition in their weddings as an homage to their past. Other groups practice this ritual as well, including the LGBTQ+ community, who understand it to symbolize the great leaps that our community has overcome to achieve equality.

Traditionally, when the wife jumped the broom, she was vowing to keep her home clean. It was also thought to be a test to see who would be head of the household—whoever jumped higher would be declared in charge. Beyond the sexist assumptions, the broom also held spiritual significance and was waved over the couple's heads to ward off evil spirits and sweep away anything in the past not worth keeping.

Jumping the broom today, with decorated handmade brooms, is a lovely custom and one that provides a dear memento.

READINGS

The options are endless for magnificent and meaningful prose to read at your ceremony. Asking people you might not have had space for in the wedding party, or a guest you want to honor, to deliver these readings is a great way to include them in the ceremony. Choose people whose voice carries well, who don't cough, sniffle, or clear their throat a lot, and whose very presence brings you comfort and joy.

RECOMMENDED VERSES FOR CEREMONY READINGS • I could fill a whole separate book with quotes I love for weddings—and you might even find such a book on the shelf next to this one. For detailed lists of suggestions for readings, visit equallywed.com. Here I'll just provide two powerful statements about marriage and equality that are used by many LGBTQ+ couples and their allies.

Justice Anthony Kennedy's majority opinion in the Supreme Court ruling on June 26, 2015, included these gorgeous sentiments:

> *No union is more profound than marriage, for it embodies the highest ideals of love, fidelity, devotion, sacrifice, and family. In forming a marital union, two people become something greater than once they were. As some of the petitioners in these cases demonstrate, marriage embodies a love that may endure even past death. It would misunderstand these men and women to say they disrespect the idea of marriage. Their plea is that they do respect it, respect it so deeply that they seek to find its fulfillment for themselves. Their hope is not to be condemned to live in loneliness, excluded from one of civilization's oldest institutions. They ask for equal dignity in the eyes of the law. The Constitution grants them that right. The judgment of the Court of Appeals for the Sixth Circuit is reversed. It is so ordered.*

• • •

True Love Lessons

KELLY MCDOWELL AND CARYN SCHNELLINGER

Our daughter [from Kelly's previous relationship] was about eight years old when we got married. Our daughter was Kelly's maid of honor, and we incorporated her into our vows, signifying our commitment, not only to each other, but also to our new blended family. We thought it went beautifully. Our daughter stood next to us the whole time. We even said some vows to her.

And in her ruling in the 2004 *Goodridge v. Department of Public Health* case that confirmed the legal right to marry to gays and lesbians in Massachusetts, Chief Justice Margaret H. Marshall wrote:

> *Civil marriage is at once a deeply personal commitment to another human being and a highly public celebration of the ideals of mutuality, companionship, intimacy, fidelity, and family . . . Because it fulfills yearnings for security, safe haven, and connection that express our common humanity, civil marriage is an esteemed institution, and the decision whether and whom to marry is among life's momentous acts of self-definition.*

Poet Lesléa Newman wrote "Break the Glass" for her wife and read it to her at their wedding. Its inspirational interpretation of the breaking of the glass makes for an exceptional reading at any wedding where glass will be broken.

Break the Glass
(for Mary Grace Newman Vazquez)
—Lesléa Newman

Break the glass
for even in our happiest moments

let us not forget
those who hate us
those who fear us
those who destroyed our temple
Break the glass
for that which was
is no longer
and can never be again:
our separate lives have ended
our life together has begun
Break the glass
and all that would stand
in the way of our joy:
those who hate women and lesbians
those who hate Jews and Puerto Ricans
those who hate themselves
Break the glass
and as the glass shatters
let the four winds scatter
the shards
up to the heavens
and let each become a star
so that every night
we can look up at the sky
and see how hatred can be transformed
into something beautiful
by our love
Break the glass

WRITING YOUR OWN VOWS

Your wedding vows are the ultimate personalized expression of your
commitment to each other. Traditional vows include promises to cherish and honor one another, to stay true to each other in sickness and
in health, for richer and for poorer. Many couples like to add their
own stories to these assurances, sometimes adding in humor, such as,

"I promise I will try to always be on time," or sentimental thoughts, such as, "I vow to wipe away your tears of sadness and be your biggest champion in life." Try to memorize your vows as much as possible so that you can lock eyes with your darling while you speak, making your promises all the more meaningful.

Tasks to Tackle

- Talk to each other about wedding rituals you'd like to have in your ceremony.
- Shop for or make props you'll need for the rituals.
- Assign someone to be responsible for setting up your ritual props in the ceremony space.
- Find an officiant you're comfortable with.
- Create a schedule for the ceremony.
- Write or decide on your vows.
- Assign readings to your readers.
- Learn your vows.
- Arrange for premarital counseling.
- Rehearse with your officiant.
- Schedule your wedding rehearsal.

CHAPTER ELEVEN

THE RECEPTION

The wedding reception's purpose is to celebrate your new marriage, and everything that occurs after "I do" should be a purposeful tribute. You are the hosts of the reception, as well as your parents or the close relatives or elders in your community who have acted as your parents, even if they haven't contributed financially. The hosts' duties are to put on a party where everyone feels welcome and enjoys themselves. You've gotten married, and now it's time to relax and be merry.

Of course, for everything to go smoothly at the reception, there's a lot to consider, from setting the timeline to greeting the guests, to honoring traditions and setting a few new ones of your own.

TIMELINE

Here is a sample wedding reception timeline for a 5:00 P.M. wedding ceremony:

6:00 P.M.

- The cocktail reception begins no later than thirty minutes after your ceremony ends (during which time family, wedding party, and couple portraits can be made and the couple can take a few moments to themselves) and lasts forty-five minutes to an hour.

6:45 P.M.

- The couple, the attendants, and the family members join the cocktail reception.
- The banquet manager or wedding planner lets everyone know that the reception space is now open.

7:00 P.M.

- The wedding guests select their escort cards and then enter the reception space to find their table.

7:10 P.M.

- The wedding party and the couple line up in a special area outside of a preselected door.
- The DJ or bandleader gets everyone's attention.
- A spotlight might even be turned toward the special area.
- The attendants are announced by name as they enter. (It's a fun touch to have background music for them to walk in to.)
- The couple is announced by their married names. (Make sure your emcee knows how to pronounce your names and how you want to be announced.)

7:15 P.M.

- The DJ or band immediately begins the first dance song, and the guests gather around to watch you have your first dance as a married couple.

7:30 P.M.

- Guests take their seats as dinner service begins.
- During dinner, toasts are made by significant family members, honor attendants, and the couple themselves.

8:00 P.M.

- After thirty to forty-five minutes of time to eat, the couple cuts their wedding cake. (This is the signal that older guests and people with children are waiting for before they head home.)
- Other traditions can be worked into the schedule at this point, such as dances with certain parents, a bouquet toss, garter removal and tossing, or other rituals and specific dances, such as the hora or the dollar dance.

8:20–11:30 P.M.

- Dancing, mingling, and celebrating!

. . .

TOASTS

Being toasted and hearing speeches at your wedding reception is one of the best parts of the event. It's customary to serve Champagne at this time, but a refill of everyone's wineglasses is fine too. Have your wait staff pass out flutes or wineglasses filled with sparkling water or cider for the nondrinkers in your crowd. The toasts typically happen after the first course is served at dinner—or, if you're having a buffet or food stations, about twenty minutes into eating time.

WHO TOASTS? • Traditionally, if you have a wedding party, the honor attendants start the toasting. The one who begins the toasting takes the microphone from the DJ or bandleader (or stands up at their table and clinks a fork on the Champagne glass). Then both honor attendants make toasts to the couple. Next, the parents of the couple—or the significant family members or important community elders who love the couple as parents—toast the pair. When you're the one being toasted, it's proper to simply smile and say thank you; in other words, don't drink to yourself.

Next, the couple might individually toast each other, and then stand together to take turns toasting their parents and families. The floor can then be opened up to more speeches, or the DJ or bandleader can start

Mingle with everyone at your wedding! Greeting your guests is of the utmost importance. It might seem like common sense, but it's an etiquette rule often overlooked by younger newlyweds with a large group of their friends at the wedding. Whether you have a formal receiving line or go from table to table with your partner, see to it that you individually thank every person for coming. It can be far too easy to get caught up in making sure that everything is going well and that you're having the best night ever with your friends, but don't ignore the older guests. Everyone should be treated with equal significance and honored with at least a minute of your time. They know you have more people to talk to, but they'll appreciate a moment with the newlyweds.

the dinner music up or begin the dancing music. It's also totally fine to mix up the order of who toasts—or to skip toasts altogether.

THE GUEST BOOK

While not necessary, laying out a guest book at the reception can make for a thoughtful token after the wedding. Alternatives include providing cards on which guests can write notes, or a framed picture of you and your spouse with a mat around it that guests can sign. Some couples adapt the Quaker wedding certificate tradition to their own wedding where at the reception all guests sign a canvas or paper on which the couple's vows and declarations have been printed. This stays true to the idea that wedding guests are witnesses to the commitment made in the marriage. It's a wise idea to have someone managing the guest book table to encourage guests throughout the evening to stop by and write a line or two of congratulations or marriage blessings.

DANCING

Most wedding receptions involve at least a little dancing, but the level involved depends largely on your personality, the time of day the wedding is held, and, sad to say, whether alcohol is being served. Liquid courage is real, and most social drinkers depend on a little nip and sip to get their mojo going.

The couple's first dance is a time for the guests to watch and applaud as the newlyweds sway slow and steady, or break out into a choreographed number. The choice is yours. Some couples skip the first dance for a variety of reasons, and that's your prerogative. If you're having a first dance, it can begin immediately after you're introduced at the beginning of the reception (so that anyone can dance when they're finished with dinner) or as dessert is served.

Just after the couple's dance is the second dance, which traditionally involves the couple and their parents in any combination. The couples can also dance with their honor attendants at this time, or with other significant people such as grandparents or siblings. Toward either the end of this dance or the beginning of the next song, other guests are invited to dance. People skip the second dance all the time, so if you don't want to do it, just tell your DJ or bandleader ahead of time.

If you are doing special dances with anyone significant, it can be especially meaningful to select songs in advance. Even if the song isn't announced to everyone, you'll know why it's the right song for you two to share.

CLASSIC TRADITIONS EXPLAINED (BUT NOT REQUIRED)

CUTTING THE CAKE • Cutting the cake is a cherished moment at most weddings. Look to your banquet captain for managing the timing. The cake cutting is the modern-day cue to your guests that if they need to leave and not party the entire night, this is their time. For seated dinners, the cake will be cut when dessert is served, but for receptions involving buffets, food stations, or standing-only cocktail receptions, it might happen later in the event.

Anniversary Dance

The anniversary dance is a fun tradition that throws the spotlight onto other guests and lets them give you a bit of advice. For the anniversary dance, the DJ or bandleader typically invites all couples to dance on the floor. After a short period of time, they instruct the couples who have been married less than a year to leave the floor . . . then couples who've been married less than two years . . . less than five years . . . less than ten years, and so on . . . until the couple married for the longest time remains and everyone applauds them. A speech from this couple might follow after the DJ or bandleader brings them a microphone and asks them the secret to a long and happy marriage.

Wedding cakes take time to cut and serve after the couple does their initial cutting, so make sure you start the process with this in mind. Generally, the cake-cutting ceremony is announced by the DJ or bandleader, and the couple makes their way to the cake table by themselves, or accompanied by their attendants. The guests gather around to watch.

If you have a special cake knife to use, such as a new gift or a family heirloom, make sure it's already at the cake table. Traditionally, one of you will put a hand on the handle of the cake knife first, and then the other one will place a hand on top. Cutting into the bottom tier (the best one to cut), make easily removable slices by making three cuts to create two slices. Remove one small slice onto a plate, lift it up with two forks, and feed each other a bite. This ceremonial activity sweetly signifies that you'll continue to support, love, and nourish each other.

Smashing the cake in each other's faces is entirely up to you, but many couples forgo this tradition, which might even stain your wedding attire. If you're going to do it, make sure you're both on the same page so that flashes of anger don't overshadow the moment.

After the first bites are taken, a loving kiss is shared, and the photos are finished, the catering staff may wheel the cake away for mass cutting, and then the wait staff will bring out plates of cake for all the guests. If you're having a more informal wedding or a home wedding, the cake might be cut in the presence of the guests, who can then pick up their own plate of cake. If you want to save the top tier, remember to let the cake-cutting team know so that they'll immediately store it away.

TOSSING THE BOUQUET(S) • If you're carrying a bouquet, you might want to do the traditional bouquet toss. Use either your real bouquet or a toss bouquet made by your florist specifically for this occasion. Two bouquets can be tossed at the same time or in succession. The idea is to have unmarried people gather behind the person tossing the bouquet to try to catch it. Legend has it that whoever catches it will be the next to get engaged.

THROWING THE GARTER • If a garter is worn by one or both of the marriers, the other one can make a big show of having the garter wearer sit down on a chair in the middle of a group of (usually) unmarried adults. The partner then removes the garter and tosses it to the crowd. The one who catches it is destined to be the next person to get engaged.

ENDING ON A GOOD NOTE

THE SEND-OFF • Even though modern couples aren't typically heading straight to the airport or the train station—the scenario for which traditional send-offs were created—it's still fun to have a ceremonial good-bye. Some couples change into more casual clothing, but many stay in their wedding attire so as not to miss the grand photo opportunity this activity presents.

If your car or other getaway vehicle is being decorated, attendants and siblings usually have sneaked out and written "just married" on it with shaving cream (or something else that's easily washable) or tied cans with string to the bumper. When the newlyweds are ready to leave, the guests form two lines for them to run through to get into the waiting car (or golf cart, or boat, or bicycle-drawn carriage). The guests toss something biodegradable and bird/animal/insect-friendly, such as flower petals, birdseed, or paper confetti (*not* rice), or they blow bubbles, wave wands with long ribbons in multiple colors, or hold sparklers (if sparklers are safe and venue-approved).

SAFETY • Having taxi drivers waiting outside toward the end of your reception is a favor to your guests who may have overconsumed (and to the rest of the people on the road). Also, if you provided a bus, private car service, or other transportation to the wedding and reception from your host lodgings, remember to arrange for return transportation.

CLEANUP DUTIES • Cleaning up is the last thing you want to worry about after celebrating your marriage, so plan ahead and assign the cleanup chores to staff, friends, family, and some vendors. Be clear with everyone about what you want handled (including gifts, food, drink, cake, and flowers), where everything needs to go, and who is responsible for closing the venue.

THE AFTER-PARTY

If you're having the time of your life with your loved ones, you probably don't want the party to end with the reception. The after-party has become a staple of the wedding night agenda. This gathering can be either impromptu or planned. If your venue allows for it, you can return after your send-off to dance the night away with your best buds—and even have your caterer bring out a late-night offering of food, shots, bottles of Champagne, cigars—or even a midnight-style breakfast of waffles, doughnuts, and all things bacon. Or all interested in keeping the party going can head to the bar of the hotel where most guests are staying, or hit a karaoke bar or any other establishment open late into the night. (Typically, the honor attendants research possible after-party venues and arrange for the couple's drinks to be taken care of by subtly collecting money from the attending guests.)

Tasks to Tackle

- Decide if your reception will begin with a cocktail party.
- Decide if you'll do your portraits before the wedding or during the cocktail hour.
- Decide how you want to be announced by your MC. Make sure this person practices pronouncing your name if it's challenging.
- Decide if your cake cutting is going to end with smashing cake on each other's faces.
- Practice your toasts.
- Decide if you want to have a first and second dance.
- Decide if you'd like to do any other dances, and be sure the music leader knows what to play.
- Go over the order of the reception events with your staff or team.
- Decide if you'll be tossing bouquet(s) and/or garter(s).
- Prepare the send-off elements and assign someone to gather people and props and get the photographer's attention.
- Make sure your photographer has a full shot list, including the special moments you want photographed.

CHAPTER TWELVE

FOOD AND DRINK

Your wedding reception menu gives you a chance to show off your tastes as a couple. In this chapter you'll find everything you need to consider when planning the menu for your wedding reception, as well as custom fare for your rehearsal dinner, the morning-after breakfast, and any other special parties surrounding your wedding. As you'll see, you have a wide range of choices when it comes to providing your guests with delicious, visually appealing, and well-made food.

For epicurean couples, this is their favorite part of the planning. Considering your food and drink options isn't just about nourishing your guests (though they'll be awfully grateful that you are feeding them). The menu is also another key element in personalizing your wedding, adding artistic embellishments, and honoring your histories. From the first nibbles and sips passed out at cocktail hour to the dessert station, the food and beverages you offer tell a story about you, your culture, your families, and your future.

Food has long been a key element in celebrations, and your wedding day is the ultimate reason to celebrate. You've invited your wedding guests to join in on the party not just so they can ooh and aah over the showy scene you've created, but to entertain and take care of them too. If you view your wedding reception as a symbiotic event where everyone will come away feeling amazing, you're well on your way to planning a wonderful party.

HIRING A CATERER

Depending on your venue, the caterer is probably the person who is going to bring your vision to life—or help you to have a vision in the first place. When hiring a caterer, you should consider their reputation, the aesthetics of their food (check out their online portfolio), their familiarity with weddings, their food style, and, of course, the tastiness of their food.

Start by looking online and speaking to friends and your other wedding vendors. Your venue might also have a preferred catering company. Try to approach the task of hiring a caterer with a bird's-eye view. If you already know that you'll be serving a seated five-course dinner centered on Indian dishes, then narrow your search to Indian caterers (and restaurants) rather than making the search more difficult by asking a traditional and contemporary American caterer what Indian dishes they can make.

MEETING YOUR CATERER

Thanks to people who have pretended to be a couple scouting wedding caterers just to scalp a free meal, most caterers now charge for a tasting of their food (but you can request that the cost be deducted from your final bill). Usually, you'll have a chance to preselect the menu items you'd like to sample on the day of your tasting. Go online and view the choices, or ask the caterer to email them to you. Many caterers also provide wedding cakes. If you're not hiring a separate cake designer, you might do your cake tasting on the same day.

Before your meeting, sit down with your partner and make a list of the dishes that are significant to you and your family (maybe your grandmother's lasagna, or your partner's take on pineapple upside-down cake), as well as the food you've loved on restaurant dates or ideas you've gleaned from magazines and websites. The two of you can even make an online vision board to share on your tablet during the meeting with the caterer.

Other information your caterer will ask for at the meeting includes:

• Wedding date and time
• Reception venue

To Have and to Hold

When selecting passed hors d'oeuvres, go for the "sure to delight" rather than the obscure sushi roll that needs to be explained. Also, hold up each food item with one hand and attempt to eat it while also holding a cocktail or a glass of wine. If this isn't an easy feat, move on to the dish that is. Happy guests make for a fun reception.

- Description of the kitchen space of the venue (Is it full-service? Are there restrictions?)
- Approximate number of people to be served (including the wedding guests, both adults and children, and the vendors you'll be feeding—usually the musicians, DJ, videographers, and photographers)
- Your budget

Depending on the size and capacity of the catering company, they're likely to provide not only food and beverages but also the wedding cake, serving staff, barware, tableware, flatware, tables, chairs, and linens. The caterer might even be your source for renting the dance floor, tents, and other rentals.

Don't sign the contract, however, until you've done your due diligence. Catering contracts are some of the hardest to get out of without paying a hefty fine. If you can, speak with couples who have recently used the caterer you're considering, as well as other wedding vendors. How has their past service been? Did they set up on time? Was the food as good as it was at the tasting, if not better? Was the staff pleasant to the guests?

QUESTIONS TO ASK THE CATERER
- Do you use organic ingredients?
- Do you use local ingredients?

- Do you allow for variations on dishes?
- What are your most popular dishes?
- Will you share contact information with one or two of your past couples whom we can contact for referrals? *The way the food tastes and the manners of the catering staff are two things that will affect the way your wedding is remembered. Make sure you are armed with the most solid information about the company you're hiring.*
- Have you ever catered an LGBTQ+ wedding? When?
- Tell me about your diversity training for your staff. *Having a gay-friendly chef means nothing if the banquet captain is going to scoff at your queer friends or the bartender is likely to snub a transgender woman asking for a glass of Champagne. Everyone on staff needs to be on board with your wedding guests being treated equally well.*
- What are your service options for food? For drinks? *Now is the time to mention that you want a Champagne welcome for guests at the ceremony, with more Champagne passed out for the wedding toasts, whether you want food stations or a plated dinner, and so on.*
- If the food isn't prepared on-site, how is it transported?
- Will your chef prepare a family recipe for us?
- Can we bring in special dishes of our own? Will your team present them in your serving ware? *Some couples like to have family or friends bring in something specific to their relationship or their child-hood, such as a favorite dessert or entrée.*
- What will be your timing schedule for offering cocktails after the ceremony?
- How soon are appetizers brought out? *Ten to fifteen minutes into the cocktail hour is ideal.*
- Can you ensure that there will be enough staff to maintain circulation of fresh trays of food throughout the cocktail hour? *Some of your wedding party might miss the first few passes while getting photos taken with you.*
- What are the components of your typical place setting?
- What are the choices for linens? *Don't just view a photo. Be sure to see and touch them.*

- Can we bring in our own alcohol for your staff to serve? *This can cut your cost considerably because your liquor store will give you a bulk discount.*
- What are your chair choices? *Ask to see their chairs.*
- Can you provide a separate children's menu?
- Is insurance for china and crystal breakages included? If not, what is the cost of this?
- Who will oversee the cake service after we cut the cake?
- Will there be a catering manager on-site to oversee the entire event?
- What will the catering staff wear at the wedding?
- What happens to the food after the reception? *Some couples like to donate the leftovers to homeless shelters. Whatever your desire, make sure you have a conversation about it now. If it's important to you, always get it in writing.*
- What happens to the leftover liquor after the wedding? *If you've provided it, a designated friend or your planner should gather all the liquor and save it for you. If you've paid for a certain amount to be provided at your reception and some is left over, now is the time to negotiate how to retrieve what you've paid for or how you'll be charged for open bottles of liquor if they're not completely consumed.*
- What does your bar setup look like? *You'll want it to be draped completely so that no ice buckets, coolers, or surplus supplies are visible.*
- Do we need to hire a bartender or will you provide one? *If you have to hire your own bartender, make sure they have liability insurance.*
- How many bartenders do you recommend for my guest count?
- When will the bar open?
- When will the bar close?
- How will we be charged for soft bar items, such as soda, bottled water, and juice?

EAT, DRINK, AND GET MARRIED!

Feeding your guests drives up the cost of your wedding more than anything else. It's not just the food, though—it's the entire catering bill, which includes all the supplies, the service, and the alcohol. You can have a dry wedding—or as some people call it, a sober wedding—or you can stick to just beer and wine; another option is to add liquor selectively. If you decide against having any alcohol, consider having your wedding in the earlier part of the evening or the afternoon—unless most of your wedding guests would also enjoy a sober wedding. Then by all means go all out with juice and soda and mocktails.

If you're serving alcohol, there's the perennial question of how much you'll need. Every wedding guru and website seems to have a magic chart to help you make this calculation, but it's really about knowing your own guests. The majority of your crowd might be oenophiles, or martini lovers, or beer connoisseurs. You want enough to go around so that every adult guest can have at least four or five drinks, from cocktail hour to the end of the reception. And this doesn't include the Champagne toast. (If you're trying to save money, the Champagne toast would be an easy expense to cut. You can just serve whatever wine you're pouring instead. You'll quickly unload several hundreds or more from your spreadsheet, depending on what type of bubbles you were hoping to serve.) See the guide to Champagne on the following page.

One standard wine bottle pours out five glasses of vino. Champagne bottles yield about six or seven flutes of bubbly, depending on who's pouring. With liquor, you'll get about twenty cocktails per liter. Unless you go with growlers, you can easily account for how many beer bottles will be needed per the number of known beer drinkers in the crowd. Also, remember some guests will switch in the middle of the evening, moving from liquor or wine to beer.

A signature cocktail remains a favorite at weddings, and it's easy to see why. Not only does it give you another chance to put your stamp on the reception, but it also can be a major cost-saver if it's the only liquor option you supply. If you do offer a specialty drink, keep the following tips in mind:

- Make sure the bartenders are all given an exact recipe, including the kind and brand of ingredients you want used as well as the method.
- Assign someone, whether a friend or your stationer, to create a sign for the bar telling people what the special beverage is and why it's

Cheers to Champagne!

Whether your guests are going to be greeted with a flute of bubbly at the ceremony or toasting you during the reception (or both!), deciding on the type of Champagne that best suits most people is key.

The word "Champagne" is not an umbrella term for all sparkling wine—it specifically denotes sparkling wine made in the Champagne region of France and produced under specific rules for the méthode champenoise. In other parts of the world, sparkling wines go by different names (and production methods), such as prosecco in Italy and cava in Spain.

CHAMPAGNE FLAVOR PROFILES

Brut: Dry, not sweet

Extra dry: Sweet

Extra brut: Extra dry

Blanc de blancs: Made exclusively from Chardonnay grapes, this option has a delicate and light taste.

NV (nonvintage): Champagne that doesn't have a year attached to it was made from grapes from multiple years and is generally less expensive than vintage.

Rosé: Whether your rosé is made from a tiny bit of red wine poured into the blend or from macerated red grape skins, there is a major scale for sweetness in rosés. Before you buy in bulk, buy one or two bottles to taste at home.

Vintage: The rule for vintage is that the wines must be made from grapes at least 85% of which are from one year. The resulting consistency in the blend is what makes it pricier.

significant. After all, why go to the trouble of renaming your rum and coke the "Ron and Cole" if no one is going to see the name and learn how you simultaneously ordered that drink on your first date?

- Keep in mind that some guests will still ask for variations of your drink with the liquor and mixers available.

TAKE YOUR SEAT

Seating your guests is like putting together a beautiful puzzle. The challenge is equal parts science and art. There are relationships to think about (both old and new), your goals for the evening, and any special needs of some of your guests, such as the elderly or the disabled.

TABLE ARRANGEMENTS

The Sweetheart Table • The couple gets their own table during the meal. It's regal, romantic, and utterly charming, and it gives them a certain amount of privacy while they attempt to eat at least a few bites of food before circulating through the crowd again. However, if you don't enjoy being the center of attention—especially while eating— you might find this arrangement awkward.

The Wedding Party Table • A classic option for large or small weddings, a wedding party table is typically a long rectangular table alongside one of the walls or sides of the reception area. Everyone seated at this table faces out toward the rest of the guests. The couple is centered in the middle, then attendants on either side in the same order they stood in the ceremony. (If there's space, their spouses or significant others and their children sit here as well.)

The Parents' Tables • If your parents—or people who love you like parents—are attending your wedding, they might enjoy hosting their own tables. These tables customarily include family members, close friends, and parents of their children's friends who were invited. (If you invited your best friend from third grade, you might also invite their parents.) If there are too few people for two tables, seat everybody at one.

This arrangement provides a nice way for your parents to get to know each other even better now that they're connected through your marriage. However, divorced families might feel more comfortable at tables of their own.

Informal Seating for the Wedding Party • Even if you want to sit among your guests, make sure that you and your wedding party have formally assigned seats where you can rest for a moment, sip some water (yes, H_2O is your friend tonight!), and eat a few bites of food. If you're having stations or a buffet, ask a friend or a waiter to bring you both full plates of food that you can graze on.

The Guest Tables • Matching guests to the right seats involves diplomacy and strategy. Think of this as a fun task and try not to let it be too stressful. If arranging your guests' seating doesn't feel important to you, keep in mind that often at weddings with no seating assignments guests mill about feeling lost, not wanting to take up space at someone's family table. You're doing your guests a favor by showing them where to sit. But if assigning seats stresses you out, you needn't do it. (That applies to everything in this book, by the way.)

Still, your mixing and matching of personalities on your seating charts can give your guests a delightful way to meet new people. It's also a sly way of taking care of your single friends. (Many romantic matches light up at weddings!)

Here are a few strategies for seating your wedding guests:

- Keep the adults together. Most single people don't enjoy being seated with children, unless they are their own, and even if they do, they'll feel like they've been chosen to be the babysitter.
- As a general rule, keep generations together as groups. Young children should be seated with their parents. Older children and teenagers typically want their own table.
- Put couples and close friends together. If there are a few singles you want to match up in case sparks might fly, now's an

opportunity to increase their chances of having at least a conversation or catching each other's eye.

- Keep different abilities in mind. People with hearing and visual challenges will want to be seated closer to where the toasts are being made. Those who use wheelchairs will need to have a place at a table with no chair and with easy in-and-out access. Elderly and pregnant guests, as well as those with sensory disorders, might want to be far away from the speakers and the bands—and closest to the bathrooms.

LET'S FIND OUR SEAT • Whether you assign seats, put a name card at each guest's place, or allow your guests to choose their own seats at an assigned table, the overall idea is to have a seat-finding system in place so that when guests enter the reception they are not left fending for themselves. Guests who attend multiple weddings may expect a seating system, and guests who don't have experience in this usually appreciate the guidance. Keep in mind that though you're hosting the event, you won't have time to show everyone what to do and where to sit. Adults can fend for themselves if they need to, but a seating system makes the event less stressful—even if there's a bit of stress in planning it out.

· · ·

Tasks to Tackle

- Research caterers.
- Schedule initial meetings with caterers.
- Attend caterers' tastings.
- Decide what type of food and alcohol you want to serve.
- Find out if you need to hire your own bartenders.
- Determine with your caterer all the rentals you will need (linens, chairs, tables, etc.)
- Determine who will handle the leftover food and drink at the end of the reception.
- Review and sign a contract with your caterer that includes final details of the menu and itinerary.
- If you're bringing in any food, recipes, or alcohol of your own, decide how, when, and to whom it will be delivered.
- Create menus for the food and drink.
- Start working on your seating chart.

CHAPTER THIRTEEN

DESSERT

Modern traditions abound for LGBTQ+ couples' weddings and the sweet ending provided by a dessert. Whatever your sweet tooth desires, of course! Pies are on the rise at wedding receptions, and cupcake displays seem to have earned a permanent spot on the roster. DIY and caterer-created tables of an assortment of sugary and tart indulgences create a happy hum among wedding guests. And then, of course, there's the classic confection: the wedding cake.

EASY AS PIE

A crisp butter-laden crust with an incredible filling of fruit or other sweet decadence is tempting to most. But what else is it about pies that makes us so happy? They are the epitome of comfort food. Whether you choose in-season fruits, a vegetable such as pumpkin or sweet potato, or another favorite, serving pies at your wedding is a nice way to make a personal imprint.

You can have your caterer whip up some pies, buy a few at a local bakery, or even have family and friends bake and bring them. Pies are especially fitting at wedding receptions held at farms, churches, or historic buildings or in backyards or barns. Increase their cozy appeal by presenting them on varying heights of cake pedestals and placing mix-and-match printed dishes around for easy plating.

BE A CAKE CHARMER

Most every guest, no matter their age, looks forward to the wedding cake, the gorgeous complement to any reception. Whether it's an ornate ten-layer tower of frosty ivory confectionery with gold piping and powder-blue drapings or a naked two-layer cake with a crown of edible flowers, your wedding cake should fit both your venue and your wedding style, as well as your personalities. There are seemingly endless options for flavors, colors, decorations, fillings, and icings, but what really matters when it all comes together is that you love the way it looks and that it's delicious.

Some couples consider skipping the wedding cake altogether if they don't care personally for cake, but do remember that older people see the cake cutting as their cue to scuttle on home to their warm beds. If you want not just a cake but additional desserts, set up a sweets table with a single-layer wedding cake made for cutting, then turn it over to the children for eating. You'll make them feel quite special.

If you're leaning toward offering a wedding cake, take advantage of the extensive amount of information available on styles, designs, tastes, and sizes. Here's a lesson in the wedding cake vernacular so you can talk like a pro when you're speaking to the pros.

GLOSSARY OF CAKE TERMS

- **Appliqué**: A design rolled out of sugar paste and applied to fondant icing.
- **Basket weave**: A piping technique that features interwoven vertical and horizontal lines.
- **Beading**: A border along the edge of tiers that resembles tiny pearls.
- **Buttercream**: A smooth, creamy icing that stays soft so it's easy to cut through. It can be colored and/or flavored. Buttercream is also used to create piping, swags, and other borders, as well as decorative rosettes. It can be used as filling too.
- **Cake jewelry**: Bling for your wedding cake such as monograms made out of metal, Swarovski crystal, plastic, or glass.
- **Cornelli**: An elaborate piping technique that yields a squiggly or lacelike pattern.

- **Crystalized flowers**: Edible flowers preserved with sugar.
- **Dragées**: Round, edible sugar balls coated with silver or gold and used for decorative purposes.
- **Fondant**: A sweet, elastic icing made of sugar, corn syrup, and gelatin that's rolled out and draped over a cake. It's a smooth, firm base for gum-paste flowers, decorative details, and architectural designs, and it has a porcelain finish.
- **Ganache**: A sweet, rich chocolate used for icing or filling that is denser than mousse but not as dense as fudge.
- **Gum paste**: This paste of sugar, cornstarch, and gelatin is used to mold realistic-looking fruits and flowers that garnish a cake. Gum-paste decorations are edible and will last for years as keepsakes, but some say they don't taste as yummy as marzipan.
- **Latticework**: A crisscross piping detail with an open pattern.
- **Marzipan**: A paste made of ground almonds, sugar, and egg whites used to mold edible flowers or fruit to decorate the cake. Marzipan can also be rolled in sheets, like fondant, and used as icing.
- **Petal dust**: A nontoxic powder that adds sparkle or sheen to a cake.
- **Pillars**: These separators used in a tiered cake can be made of plastic or wood in several lengths to achieve the desired look. Thicker pillars are sometimes called columns.
- **Piping**: A decorative technique created using a pastry bag and various metal tips. Piping details include leaves, borders, basket-weave patterns, and flowers.
- **Pulled sugar**: A technique in which boiled sugar is manipulated and pulled to produce flowers and bows.
- **Royal icing**: Made of egg whites and confectionery sugar, this icing starts life as a soft paste piped from a pastry bag to create latticework, beading, bows, and flowers.
- **Swiss dot**: A piping technique that forms tiny dots in random patterns.
- **Tier**: When pillars or columns separate the layers of the cake rather than frosting or filling, these layers are referred to as tiers. This distinction is important when ordering a cake.

- **Torte**: A dense cake.
- **Whipped cream**: Heavy cream beaten to achieve a thick consistency.

CHOOSING YOUR CAKE MAKER • Wedding cakes have a way of becoming the main stars of the wedding reception, and for good reason. They can be dressed up in a myriad of ways, from ornate sugar flowers to metallic edible paints. When hiring the wedding cake designer who'll be creating your celebratory confection, meet in person—or at least on the phone rather than by email alone—to discuss the following points:

- Have you ever worked with an LGBTQ+ couple before? *Plenty of bakeries and pastry chefs have made the news over their refusal to work with LGBTQ+ couples. Better to ask up front what a cake maker's comfort level and experience is. If you're a butch/femme couple, you might want a groom's cake for your masculine partner. Some two-groom couples opt for two groom's cakes. These choices are entirely up to you, and it's not only imperative that your cake decorator know that you're in charge, but also that they make sincere suggestions based on you as a couple, not just on what they're used to doing.*
- How is your pricing established? Do you have a per-slice charge, or do you charge extra for certain designs?
- How long before the wedding do you make the cakes? Do you freeze them beforehand or keep them fresh?
- Are all your ingredients natural and made in-house?
- Do you have a delivery charge, and if so, how much?
- If I have fresh flowers going on my cake, who will place them on the cake at the venue: you or the florist?
- Can you provide me with a sketch or photo of the cake I'm ordering, along with a written description of both the interior and exterior?

STYLING YOUR CAKE • One way to tie your cake to your venue is through your theme, season, or location. For a fall wedding, consider a neutral color palette with one or two large seasonal flowers, such as dahlias. If you're marrying in a modern wedding venue, such as a hotel ballroom or an art gallery, think about a classic-looking wedding cake with sleek monogrammed initials on the top. If you're having an outdoor wedding, a boho wedding cake with wildflowers and minimal frosting would work. Two grooms getting married sometimes have a desire for a less feminine wedding cake. Using descriptive words such as "architectural," "sleek," "graphic," and "handsome" may help you convey your wishes to your baker. New York cake master Ron Ben-Israel frequently makes phenomenal cakes for same-sex couples, including some that have fewer flowers and play more to the grooms' interests, such as sailing or diving.

In hetero weddings, the bride often surprises the groom with a groom's cake. This sweet gift unveiled at the wedding reception is usually cut by the staff and is not part of the traditional cake-cutting ceremony. Some LGBTQ+ couples skip this tradition altogether and just have one wedding cake. Others opt for two groom's cakes with different design elements but of the same size, so that neither outshines the other. For butch/femme couples, there might be one star wedding cake and another called a "broom's cake." The same element of surprise can be brought to the broom's cake, with one partner unveiling to the other a distinctive cake that's often far too specialized to be a wedding cake. The cake's theme could be anything from sports or a favorite book to an homage to a type of animal.

MIND YOUR BUDGET • Wedding cake is usually priced by the slice. The cost can vary, but it generally ranges from $3 to $25 a slice (and beyond). It's easy to be wooed by toasted coconut and banana filling and a multi-flavor cake when you're making decisions with sugar rushing to your head. Having a handle on your budget—and knowing what will affect it—will allow you to prioritize your choices: more flavors equals more money; the more complicated the flavor, the bigger the price tag; handmade sugar flowers will add dollars to every slice; and fondant icing is generally more expensive than buttercream.

Sweet Talk

GUEST EXPERT: RON BEN-ISRAEL
Ron Ben-Israel Cakes, New York City

The range of cakes we have designed for same-sex couples is as varied and unique as the celebrants themselves. Some are interested in a more traditional-looking cake; for them, the act of legally getting married is statement enough. Still others seek to incorporate their personalities and taste sensibilities into the cake, and therefore we devote extensive time to the design process for every wedding. Each cake is the product of dialogue and expression between our bakers and the happy couple—it represents their partnership, and this can be shown in any number of ways. For one couple, I made a cake with two sugar trees intertwined at the top. For another, one from San Francisco and one from New York, I made a cake with landmarks of both cities.

When planning your dream cake, any descriptive words can help a baker, but visuals are much better than labels. I always recommend that couples bring to their consultation anything related to the reception. That can be flowers, linen, centerpieces, photos of the venue, invitations, or clothing. Since the cake is a celebration of your union, consider your mutual pasts and interests—inspiration can be found anywhere.

When it comes to decoration, adornment costs run the gamut. Perhaps the most inexpensive option is fresh organic fruits or flowers. However, fresh flowers need to be verified as organic and nonpoisonous before placed anywhere near food. Even if your florist is providing the cake topper, have them work with the baker to ensure that the flowers are safe and clean enough for your cake. On the high end are delicate gum-paste or sugar-paste flowers, which are constructed by hand, one petal at a time. But here's the bottom line: all add-ons—including marzipan fruits, chocolate-molded flowers, and lace points—will raise the cost.

SIZE MATTERS • Match your cake size to your wedding reception space. Generally, three layers will serve 50 to 100 guests; you'll probably need five layers for 200 guests or more. Your cake should fit the space too—if your reception is in a grand ballroom, consider increasing the cake's stature with columns between the tiers, or opting for a faux Styrofoam layer (no one will know!) to add height.

CHOOSING A FLAVOR • Besides being a masterpiece, you'll want your cake to taste good too. It's important to choose the flavor *you* want, not what you think everyone else wants. When you meet with prospective bakers, taste lots of flavors. Don't be afraid to stray from vanilla and chocolate. And don't forget to sample fillings too—many bakers enjoy working with complicated flavorings, like guava and mango or hazelnut and mocha.

WEATHER IS EVERYTHING

If you're having an outdoor wedding in a hot climate, watch out for whipped cream, meringue, and buttercream, which melt when it gets too hot. Ask your baker about summer icing options or opt for a fondant-covered cake, which doesn't require refrigeration.

TOP IT OFF • Wedding cake toppers run the gamut from kitschy plastic figurines that look nothing like you to custom figurines that look *exactly* like you, to antiques such as an heirloom piece passed down through the generations that can double as your something old and your baker can usually integrate into the cake's design. Also, more companies are showing their support for same-sex couples with two-men or two-women figurines sold as couples, as well as laser-cut-out words such as "Mr. and Mr." and "Mrs. and Mrs." "Cake jewelry," a relatively new term, is bling for your wedding cake such as monograms made out of metal, Swarovski crystal, plastic, or glass. Other choices include a bouquet of sugar flowers, a waterfall of icing ribbons, or even a sugar block carved to reveal your new monogram.

Look to your locale as well. Nearly anything can become your cake's topper: a family heirloom; commissioned statues to look like you, your spouse, and any number of pets or children; your monogram in laser-cut wood, metal, or crystal; fresh flowers; sugar-paste flowers;

crystallized flowers; and fruit. A cluster of coral can look stunning for a beachside celebration, or try a fondant snowflake for a winter wedding. Or don't use a topper at all—some designs look great without it.

HAVE A DETAILED DELIVERY PLAN • Cake delivery takes coordination (and usually a refrigerated van), so give yourself peace of mind and opt to have your cake delivered. Cut another expense if you have to, but be sure to budget in the cost of delivery. Complex cakes may not necessarily arrive in final form, so allow time and space for assembly. And make sure that once the masterpiece is delivered, it has a place at the venue (especially if it requires refrigeration). Discuss all the delivery details with your baker or caterer before signing the contract. Make sure that every detail also appears in the day-of itineraries for the baker, caterer, and planner.

GAZE UPON THE GLAZE • People will want to marvel at your cake before it's cut and eaten. Have a designated, well-lit table that allows the best presentation possible. A round one is perfect for circular cakes, but a straight design may call for a rectangular table. Drape the table with luxe linens and decorate it with colors and flowers to complement the cake and motif.

CUT TO THE CAKE • Some venues charge an additional fee to cut and serve the wedding cake when a cake designer isn't affiliated with their establishment. This is a financial incentive for you to use the venue's in-house baker. If you decide to have your cake made elsewhere, factor in another $1.50 or more per person to have it cut by your venue or catering company. Want to avoid this fee altogether? Serve cupcakes.

MAKE A NOTE OF IT • Make sure your caterer gets fifteen minutes of lead time before you head over to cut the cake. Even the speediest pros in the catering business will need that much time to refill Champagne or wineglasses and ready the cake table with all the necessary cake-cutting accoutrements (such as the essential plates and forks). Also, have your emcee announce the cake cutting and make sure those with special needs and older people have time to get to the area. Many people will have been waiting for this special moment in the reception.

SMASH AND GRAB • Like the dollar dance, everyone has their own opinion about the etiquette of the cake smash—the act of smooshing cake onto your spouse's face that has become somewhat of a wedding reception tradition. If you don't want a slice of wedding cake smashed into your perfectly made-up face, we suggest a little heart-to-heart with your one and only before you cut. If you're both game to partake, have a few extra napkins on hand.

SAVING THE TOP TIER • Many couples save the top tier of their cake for their first wedding anniversary. To do this safely, remove all flowers, stems, leaves, and any other garnishes. Wrap the cake carefully in plastic and then seal it in an airtight container. Put it in your freezer and don't forget to label it—you'd be surprised how much wedding cake can look like every other frozen item after a year!

Tasks to Tackle

- Research cake makers.
- Schedule initial meetings with cake makers.
- Attend cake flavor and filling tastings.
- Determine exactly how the cake will look and taste, and finalize these details in the contract.
- Go over the cake delivery plan.
- Determine who will place the cake topper and when.

CHAPTER FOURTEEN

MUSIC AND DANCING

Music is such an important aspect of your wedding. It adds a vibration, a hum, a rhythm to every moment of the day, whether it's a slow and romantic ballad or the sashay of feet waltzing all over the dance floor late into the night to classic songs. Music creates the flow of the party and serves as a memory keeper. Years from now, when you hear songs from your ceremony and reception, you'll be transported back to your magical wedding day, hearing the soundtrack of your love story that brought your celebration to life.

Flow is essential for a fabulous wedding that will have your guests' cheeks flushed with excitement. You'll want to welcome guests to your ceremony space with an upbeat but measured music choice. Similarly, when you invite your guests to enter your reception space when the doors open, you'll want them to be caught up in the wonder and delight of it all, from the decor, to the glass of wine they're greeted with, to the immediate welcome notes of music in their ears.

Ceremony music can be provided by a plethora of potential talented sources. Many couples go for mainly instrumental beats, but some enjoy singers as well. Orchestral ensembles, guitarists, saxophonists, trombone players, or bagpipe players—the aural opportunities are endless.

For your reception music, decide if you want to have a live band, hire a DJ, or take a DIY approach courtesy of a friend and an iPod. The rich sound and spontaneous vibe of live bands make for a more interactive experience. The bandleader can adjust the tempo of the evening with different sets, from jazzy cocktail music to upbeat dance tunes. Of course, live bands usually require a larger financial investment, and the band you hire might have only one or two styles of music in its repertoire. A DJ offers more variety and, unlike a cover band, can provide the original artists singing the hits. Either way, hire your musicians well in advance. The coveted ones are booked eight to twelve months out.

If you're considering going DIY for your wedding music, the people you appoint to operate the music can make or break your sound system. Make sure you have a trusted friend or family member in charge, someone you can count on, so you're not sweating bullets the entire night during the transitions instead of enjoying your wedding.

Before you book anyone, though, understand the lineup of your wedding. Whether you're reciting your vows at city hall and having a reception back at your house, holding the ceremony and reception at a posh downtown hotel, or having a destination wedding in Maui, music is almost always incorporated into the traditional course of events as outlined in the next two sections.

CEREMONY MUSIC

1. **The prelude**: The prelude music is played while your wedding guests are being seated.

2. **The processional**: This music begins as the couple's parents or other most important people are being seated. Then, if one partner is going to be waiting at the front of the ceremony space with the officiant, with their attendants as well as the attendants for the other partner, they enter at this time and take their places. When the couple enters the ceremony space—either alone or together, a new song typically begins.

   Suggestions for prelude and processional music include:
   - "Canon in D Major" (Pachelbel)
   - "All of You" (John Legend)
   - "I Was Married" (Tegan and Sara)
   - "Air on the G String" (Johann Sebastian Bach)
   - "A Thousand Years" (Christina Perri)
   - "Hallelujah" (Leonard Cohen/Jeff Buckley)
   - "La Vie en Rose" (Edith Piaf/Andrea Bocelli)

3. **The interlude**: Interlude music is a nice way to add symbolic meaning to parts of the ceremony, such as lighting the unity candle or signing the ketubah.

   Suggestions for interlude music include:
   - "Ave Maria" (Johann Sebastian Bach/Charles Gounod)
   - "Hoppípolla" (Sigur Rós)
   - "The Water Is Wide" (traditional/James Taylor)
   - "Reverie" (Claude Debussy)

4. **The recessional:** When the ceremony is over and you've sealed the marriage with a kiss, you're deliriously happy and it's time to go celebrate. There's still order to maintain, though. Everyone except the guests traditionally walks out in the order in which they came in—even family, who are usually waiting with huge grins on their faces.

    First to walk out is the happy couple, followed by the wedding party. At this point the officiant usually makes an announcement about where to go for the cocktail party (you know, the important news). Then everyone disperses while you go have your portraits done or whatever you've decided to do at this exciting time. Congrats—you are married!

    Suggestions for recessional music include:
    - "Best Day of My Life" (American Authors)
    - "Ode to Joy" (Ludwig van Beethoven)
    - "Signed, Sealed, Delivered" (Stevie Wonder)
    - "You Make My Dreams Come True" (Hall and Oates)

5. **The postlude:** This is the music that continues as the guests make their way out of the ceremony space. It can be more of the same joyous music played during the recessional or some softer but still upbeat tunes.

RECEPTION MUSIC

Let your personality be your guidepost here. Most of your guests are coming for a full celebration of your marriage, and music is the catalyst for just such an occasion. Your music sets the tone for the event just as much as the venue does.

DAYTIME RECEPTIONS • Depending on the temperament of your guests and the style of your wedding, a daytime wedding generally calls for softer music so that conversations are the focus rather than dancing.

EVENING WEDDINGS

Cocktail Hour • While guests are mingling in this first hour, the couple and the wedding party are often taking their official wedding portraits. Because the focus is on conversation, the music should be lighter. If you had a string musician for the ceremony, consider having them stay on and keep playing for this additional time. They might even have had a minimum time that you need to meet. Or have one or two of your reception musicians come early and play light but lively jazz during this time. Instruct them to play instrumental music only, though, as it allows people to focus on their conversations rather than the stage.

May I Have Your Attention, Please? • Your entrance as the newlyweds officially marks the transition from the cocktail hour to the reception. You might want to have a song played as you walk out together. Go over music choices and how you'd like to be announced with your master of ceremonies. Mr. and Mr. Baxter-Smith? Mrs. and Mrs. Sykes? The Millers? Phil and James? The Dean family? To make sure your names are announced exactly the way you want, say it out loud to your MC, have them say it back to you, then write it down for them, including the phonetic pronunciation, and print it out on their copy of the day-of wedding itinerary (which every vendor will receive). See more on reception planning on page 102.

No matter whether you have a cover band belting out songs, a DJ playing music on a laptop, or a friend managing an iPhone, keep in mind that you don't have to suffer through hetero love songs at your own wedding. These tunes testify to queer love:

- "If I Had You" (Adam Lambert)
- "She Says" (Ani DiFranco)
- "What a Beautiful Day" (Brett Every)
- "Hold Each Other" (Chad King of A Great Big World)
- "Let's Make Love and Listen to Death from Above" (CSS)
- "So Beautiful" (Darren Hayes)

- "Forrest Gump" (Frank Ocean)
- "Too Young to Be in Love" (Hunx and His Punx)
- "She" (Jen Foster)
- "Power of Two" (Indigo Girls)
- "I Kissed a Girl" (Jill Sobule)
- "Your Song" (John Barrowman)
- "TC and Honeybear" (John Grant)
- "She's Crushing My Mind" (Kaia Wilson/Team Dresch)
- "I Think She Knows" (Kaki King/Justin Timberlake)
- "She Keeps Me Warm" (Mary Lambert)
- "Handsome Man" (Matt Alber)
- "Latch" (Sam Smith)
- "The First Time" (Matt Fishel)
- "I'm the Only One" (Melissa Etheridge)
- "Origin of Love" (Mika)
- "Real" (Olly Alexander of Years and Years)
- "Might Tell You Tonight" (Scissor Sisters)
- "Damn I Wish I Was Your Lover" (Sophie B. Hawkins)
- "Closer" (Tegan and Sara)
- "Jet Boy, Jet Girl" (Elton Motello/The Damned)
- "Papa Was a Rodeo" (The Magnetic Fields)
- "Gasoline" (Troye Sivan)

Once you have a sense how your ceremony and reception will flow, think about the style of music and musicians that makes sense for the songs you'd like to play and the announcements you'll have made, and that also will fit the logistics of your venue and what can be accommodated there.

SOUND CHECK

Find out from the officiant, music director, or site manager what type of music and instruments sound best in the space to make sure you know what the music is going to sound like. Also, be sure to investigate whether the guests will be able to hear you. If you're having a large wedding or a beach wedding, you may need to wear mics, and there should be speakers at both the front and back of the ceremony space. Find out what sound equipment is allowed in your ceremony space and add the cost of renting it to your budget and checklist—or ask your music vendors what they can provide.

RESTRICTIONS

Whether you're getting married at a church, a synagogue, a museum, or a historic site, many places have sound ordinances as well as specific rules regarding music selections. Find out what these restrictions are and be sure to relay this information to your music vendors as well as your day-of coordinator or event planner.

RESEARCHING YOUR SOUND PROVIDERS

When looking for music professionals for your wedding, start by thinking back to events with performances you've enjoyed, and not just weddings. Birthday bashes, office holiday parties, weekend festivals, and live music played at restaurants all offer opportunities to hear musicians and DJs in their element. Most of these musicians will be open to playing at a wedding—or even have experience with it.

Ask those in your social circles for recommendations of music professionals in the area. Then, if you're still coming up short, go online, where directories abound of wedding musicians, bands, and DJs vying for your business. Look for someone who can give you a chance to view their demo or even come hear them live. If they're listed as an equality-minded vendor in equallywed.com's LGBTQ+ wedding directory, all the better.

INTERVIEWING BANDS, DJS, AND MUSICIANS

Don't let yourself get intimidated by the cool vibe from the DJ or bandleader. You still need to ask some important questions.

- Have you worked with LGBTQ+ couples before?
- Are you open to creating a gender-neutral playlist? *You should be allowed to provide a "do-not-play list"—you know, like "When a Man Loves a Woman"—but you also want your DJ or bandleader to be careful about avoiding obvious hetero love songs that you might not have cleared first. Have an open dialogue with your DJ and bandleader about this.*
- What's your comfort level with changing the typical reception itinerary? *If you want to skip the father-daughter dance or other such traditions, discuss it ahead of time so your DJ doesn't commit a faux pas at the reception.*
- What are your travel fees?
- What's your backup plan if your equipment fails or you're sick on the day of my wedding?
- What kind of equipment do you have? What will you have to rent? *The familiarity of DJs and musicians with their equipment is extremely important.*
- How comfortable are you with the idea of also serving as the emcee of the evening?
- How do you pace the evening?
- How many hours of playing time are included in the contract?
- How many breaks will you take?
- What's your cancellation policy?
- Where can I see videos of you performing to get a feel for your style?
- Will you share contact information with one or two of your past couples whom we can contact for referrals?
- What do you usually wear at weddings? *Vendors should be open to dressing up or down in accordance with your wishes—within reason.*
- Will you be able to attend our rehearsal to review the timing for the ceremony music?

Tasks to Tackle

- [ ] Interview and hire musicians.

- [ ] Determine your must-play and do-not-play lists.

- [ ] Finalize and sign contracts with the musicians, bands, or DJ.

- [ ] Two to four weeks before the wedding, check in with your musician to confirm every detail.

- [ ] Don't forget to have at least one of the musicians or the DJ attend the wedding rehearsal.

CHAPTER FIFTEEN

DECOR

The name of the game with weddings is personalization—
and that applies to both your ceremony and your reception. We personalize by transforming the space to match our wedding vision. But what does that mean exactly? Think back to Chapter 5. What was it that you dreamed up when you closed your eyes? A husky hoedown under the moonlit skies with a brewery nearby? A luxurious ballroom wedding at a downtown hotel? A destination wedding in Mexico? Or Italy? Your backyard? An art gallery's covered patio transformed into a retro disco party? Once you know how you want your wedding reception to look overall, you can work backwards and pay attention to how every detail contributes to your vision. It's all in the details, no?

The general term "wedding decor" covers everything from flowers, photo backdrops, and tablescapes to the chairs, music stage, and dance floor. Keep in mind that no matter what your budget can handle, whether it's centerpieces or handmade favors, be creative and enjoy yourselves. Before we dive into the logistics of gussying up your space, let's go over who you can hire to help achieve your dreams.

FLORIST VS. EVENT DESIGNER

Hiring the right person to help you plan your reception decor can quickly become confusing. Here's the breakdown of who does what in the business:

- **Florists and floral designers**: These names and roles are similar; between them, florists and floral designers offer a wide range of flower design services. For your purposes, be sure that you find a floral professional who specializes in weddings and can expertly navigate your venue.
- **Event designers**: These professionals might use flowers in their bevy of props to execute their design of your wedding. Some florists work as wedding planners, and some event designers double as planners. Many hats are worn in the world of wedding event design—party hats, to be sure.
- **Rental companies**: As covered on page 46, rental companies are a stellar source for chairs, tables, glasses, and linens if your venue or caterer doesn't provide these items, you're a DIY couple, or your venue is unconventional. Rental companies can also offer fantastic props such as drapes for ceilings, table lamps, pillows and outdoor furniture, fun lighting, dance floors, lounges and hammocks for outdoor receptions, bars, and all sorts of other fabulous fun ideas.

Now that you have a general sense of the professionals you might call on, you can consider the bigger picture of the ceremony and reception decor that's right for you. When it comes to planning how your ceremony will look, step back and imagine it from a guest's perspective.

THE CEREMONY SPACE

As you think about decorating the ceremony space, you want to keep in mind a few fundamental questions: Am I covering all my bases? Am I also looking at the big picture? And am I working within my original vision?

The most important fundamental, however, is remembering why you're here, in this moment, in this ceremony space—because you are dedicating the rest of your life to another human being who you can't imagine being without and who feels the same way about you. The ceremony space is part of your narrative. Is it romantic and full of blooming hopeful flowers? Is it a minimalist space with richly hued green plants and smooth pebbles brimming with strength and staying power? Let your love be the guide.

WELCOME! THE ENTRY WAY • As you plan the decor for each area, pretend you're a guest. Walking into the ceremony space, you're looking for guidance. Maybe there's signage to direct you to the ceremony space. (If you like that idea, create signs that match the rest of your wedding design, whether that's a rustic painted wooden sign for your barn wedding or a flower-framed calligraphed sign for your romantic garden wedding.)

If not a sign, maybe you're greeted by an usher or two, or perhaps you quickly see a basket of programs or something else set out to say, "You've arrived!" (Your welcome table or entryway could probably use a sprig or two of something pretty. Talk to your florist about what works for this space. Plan for all your ushers and escorts to have flowers to wear on their lapel or their wrist, whichever is most comfortable for them.)

SEATING • For venues without built-in seats, other seating choices abound, from traditional chairs to pews (not just for churches! rent them for your wedding in a field), hay bales, or sofas. Typically, a florist will want to place floral arrangements such as pomander balls (those lovely flower balls that hang from a loop of ribbon) or vases of flowers down the aisle in some format, depending on the seating. If you are not using an usher, work with your florist to designate the first two rows for family or guests with special needs without resorting to a sign that could be interpreted as in poor taste. Florists know just how to handle this sensitive issue by using thin garlands of flowers to close off certain seating areas.

If there is no one escorting guests to their seat, then you might want to set up a sign that indicates which side of the ceremony space belongs to which partner. This distinction is not for the benefit of your younger guests, but to guide your older guests who are accustomed to heterosexual weddings at which the bride's family sits on the left and the groom's family sits on the right. In LGBTQ+ weddings, signs are very often placed in front of the ceremony space telling guests in a variety of clever ways that they needn't worry about where they sit (with the exception, of course, of the first few rows for family). If you're making a sign or having your calligrapher design one, popular sign messages include:

TODAY AS TWO FAMILIES BECOME ONE, WE ASK
THAT YOU CHOOSE A SEAT, NOT A SIDE.

CHOOSE A SEAT, NOT A SIDE. EITHER WAY, IT'S FOR A BRIDE.

CHOOSE A SEAT, NOT A SIDE. WE'RE ALL
FAMILY ONCE THE KNOT IS TIED.

TOGETHER FOREVER. PLEASE FEEL FREE TO SIT WHEREVER.

AN ARCH OR CHUPPAH • The wedding arch or chuppah is a canopy under which you and your partner say your vows. Arches can be meaningful in that they represent the home you are building together. They can be rented from a variety of vendors, but if you're feeling crafty, you can make one with flowers, ribbons, garland, linen, or other light fabrics. Making it together, or incorporating in to it an item of significance to you as a couple, can make your arch all the more distinctive.

A BACKDROP • Modern weddings are now including backdrops instead of or in conjunction with the arch or chuppah. If there's no gorgeous vista in the background, the masterpiece you've created yourself—whether from flowers, plants, wood, balloons, paper art, or some other creative element—often adds to the star power of your wedding photos. A backdrop also helps retain sound so that your guests can hear you better.

AN ALTAR • When you stand at the front of the ceremony space with your partner, the officiant is typically in front of you. Attendants may or may not be flanking you on either side. Draw the guests' eyes up toward the focal point of the area by placing large vases of flower arrangements on either side of the officiant. More arrangements can be added—sparingly, and with purpose—at least three feet away from this space, in any direction. (Take a look, for instance, at the sound or music section to see if it could use some sprucing up.)

THE RITUAL TABLE • If you and your partner are performing any rituals, such as a sand ceremony or unity candle lighting, don't make the mistake of having only the items you'll need to complete the ritual on a nearby table. Tend to that table as you have the rest of the wedding decor. Ask the florist to place flowers on it that can be taken back to the reception afterward. Consider adding a garland runner the length of the table.

THE AISLE(S) • Decorating the aisle can be quite simple if you want nothing on it. But modern traditions being what they are, you've got a bevy of options here, from a personalized runner to flower petals placed before the couple arrives in some kind of tiered fashion (bicolor, tricolor, etc.). Make sure you have a team member discreetly scatter the fresh petals just before you come out. As with decorating the front rows for family, your florist will have ideas on decorating the ends of the seats on the aisle.

THE WEATHER STATIONS • If your wedding is even slightly informal—and especially if it's outdoors—there are some items you can offer your guests at the beginning of the ceremony for which they will be very thankful.

Set up a drink station offering non-alcoholic premade juices, with signs welcoming guests to help themselves before they take a seat. You can decorate this area with flowers or plants on a wooden table. You could also have a team of waiters serving flutes of Champagne. (Ask your florist about single flowers or succulents for their trays.)

Depending on your venue, it may be wise to have baskets ready of less-fun but necessary goodies: mosquito repellent wipes, SPF wipes, personal fans, flip-flops in all sizes (if you're asking your guests to walk out to the beach from this point). If you decide to offer all of these items to each guest, consider placing them in stiff burlap or linen bags no larger than your hand that can be placed under the guests' chairs for the ceremony but pulled out for important times—like when it's 100 degrees with no wind, or when the mosquitoes have found their target and they've brought backup.

All of these items can be personalized with stickers showcasing your names, your wedding date, your monogram, or any other elements taken from your wedding stationery. These items can also be trotted out for the reception if the ceremony is indoors but the party is taking place outdoors.

Finally, for fall and winter weddings, some guests may very well appreciate being able to choose a warm wrap from baskets of wraps—in your wedding colors of course—by the welcome signs.

THE RESTROOMS

Decorations for the restrooms should be on your radar, not only because they provide another opportunity for personalization, but because practically all of your guests will be visiting the bathrooms at some point during your event. Make sure they're comfortable! First, consider hanging your own signs on the restroom doors to indicate that they're unisex. (Get the venue's permission and remember not to use any nails or staples.) Make the restrooms themselves a welcoming place by having monogrammed soaps and small baskets of toiletries such as hair combs, hand lotion, hand sanitizer, condoms for later, dental floss, breath mints and/or mouthwash (with small cups), hair gel, Q-tips, and makeup wipes.

A RAIN CONTINGENCY PLAN

No one wants to plan for rain on their wedding day, despite the superstition that it brings about fertility in the marriage. We're LGBTQ+. We have to pay extra for that. But the reality is that sometimes nature has its way, and you have to be ready for it. By now, however, you've become a pro at making contingency plans!

OUTDOOR WEDDINGS • If you're having an outdoor wedding, conducting the ceremony under a tent is the best insurance you'll have. However, you might not have the happy sun you envisioned fully radiating down on you. If you have the budget for it, pay in full for the outdoor tent but don't have it set up if the weather is going to hold off. The rental company usually sets up the tent the night before, so they might even give you a partial refund. The key word here is *might*. You could opt for a clear tent so you can still see the sun, but on a stifling hot day you'll surely be baking under the plastic ceiling, as it tends to have a greenhouse effect. Ideally, you'll have sunshine on your wedding day that can be seen from every angle under the canopy, and you can extend the non-tent outdoor feeling under your tent with flower and plant installations that offer a garden or forest effect.

INDOOR WEDDINGS • Even if you are having an indoor wedding, you still might imagine that your guests could go outside on the terrace for cocktail hour while your ceremony space is being transformed into the reception hall. Ask the venue whether they can offer a backup plan in the event of rain or other bad weather putting a damper on the use of this transition space.

LIGHTING

Starry-eyed lovers might be drawn to string lighting for their evening weddings, with lights strung above the guests' heads and their wedding arch. Remember your vision as you plan for lights—maybe it's Italian, rustic, and "our love has no bounds"—but be aware that a moody and low-lit wedding ceremony space with only a few candelabras, though romantic in theory, may compromise the comfort and safety of some of your guests and hamper your vendors' ability to effectively do their job. Not to mention that photos shot in semi-darkness might not be as good.

AUDIO REQUIREMENTS

Larger ceremonies often call for microphones and speakers. The DJ emceeing the ceremony jams might be able to set them up. Whatever

Keep in mind that much of your ceremony decor can—and should—be repurposed for your reception. While your guests are imbibing at the cocktail hour, your reception setup team can transport any items doing double duty to the reception space.

the case, work with your DJ, florist, and event designer to cohesively ensure that the equipment is (a) not a safety hazard to your guests (cords need to be safely and professionally taped down), and (b) capable of being incorporated into the design rather than standing in opposition to it. Dome flower arrangements on small tables on either side of a mammoth speaker stand might not look as good as two tall cylindrical vases of full, bushy hydrangeas and roses, looking as if they all belong together.

THE COCKTAIL HOUR

If you're having a cocktail hour in a location separate from your ceremony and reception, there are more decor items to consider. For instance, the cocktail hour presents another opportunity for a welcome sign, especially if you didn't use one at the wedding ceremony. Deciding whether to have signage signifying where the cocktail hour will take place depends on its distance from the site of the ceremony and on how much of a time delay there'll be between the two events. For example, some wedding ceremonies take place at three o'clock in the afternoon and the reception doesn't begin until six.

The cocktail hour is typically the time when guests get a little more relaxed with liquid courage so as to give you their best on the dance floor or with a fun toast. The decor and entertainment here ought to provide a small taste of what they'll get when they walk into your reception space. You can have passed trays of hors d'oeuvres, an open bar (another chance to decorate with flowers or succulents, as well as personalized cocktail napkins, matches, and paper straws in your wedding colors), or, keeping it simple, multiple rotating staff with trays of wine and beer. Respect the choice of some guests not to drink by also offering a fun mocktail (a creative non-alcoholic drink with fresh juice and mixers), juice, and water (both sparkling and still).

THE RECEPTION SPACE

The ceremony is over, you are married, and it's time to celebrate like never before!

Start by assessing which areas of your venue already have decor you want to keep and what you'll need to have brought in—and which team member will be responsible for that.

Decorating the reception space may be where you pull out all the stops—this is, after all, where 40 percent of the wedding money is typically spent—but decor opportunities here are almost always capped by budget. Decide on everything you want and need, and then cut back, rather than starting small. You might be able to slash something else in another area that is less noticeable in order to afford the burlesque dancers for your reception. Let's just find out, shall we?

THE ESCORT CARD DISPLAY • When guests enter the reception space, the first thing they do after oohing and aahing is try to find the seats for themselves and their mate, their date, or the entire troupe they RSVPed for. As discussed on page 119, I highly advise avoiding the chaos that is a reception without a seating plan. It's a courtesy to your guests to make it easy for them to walk into a room and immediately find their place. Then they can quickly start enjoying themselves! Seniors, pregnant people, and people with special needs should be seated close to the bathrooms so they won't have to worry about the distance. Keep all this in mind when you create an escort card display. Instead of setting place cards at their seats for guests to find, create an art piece of seating assignments and display it near the entrance of the reception space. For the unfamiliar, place cards direct guests to the table and the seat to which they're assigned, whereas escort cards only indicate the table at which they'll sit. You can have both an escort card display at the entry of your reception and place cards at each seat, or simply the escort cards. Of course, don't forget to mark the tables with the corresponding number or name matching what's on the escort cards.

THE GUEST BOOK • Your wedding is going to be a bit of a happy blur and ten years from now, you're not going to remember everyone who came to your wedding. It's nice to get your guests either to sign a traditional guest book or to log their presence in a more contemporary way. For more on guest books and other options, turn to page 105.

THE MUSIC CENTER • The stage, musician's stand, band, or DJ area can also be decorated (with water-free elements). Use a fun backdrop to detract from the equipment and remember that lighting, whether it's chandeliers, lanterns, or LED, can be used to create dramatic effect. Strands of garlands along the front of the bandstand or sound booth are also lovely. If you're having a full stage for musicians, speak with your caterer or venue about a stage skirt, a fabric that goes around the stage and is usually available in a variety of colors and textures.

OTHER IMPORTANT TABLES • If your guests will be serving themselves at a buffet line or separate food stations around the room, work with the venue to see if you can have them decorate the food sites with garlands of your choosing (for example, fresh greenery rather than plastic ivy).

THE GIFT TABLE • These days most guests ship their gifts ahead of time, but you can expect that there will still be some who bring their presents to the wedding and you need to have a place for those gifts to go. If you are getting married in a large venue where multiple weddings are being held on the same day, consider making label sheets available with your name, your partner's name, the wedding date, your phone numbers, and where you are staying. Place them in a cute basket on

your gift table with instructions for your guests to place one on each gift left. This way, when the person responsible collects the wedding gifts from the reception, there should be no confusion about the proper delivery of any gift that slips through the cracks.

What can make a gift table more attractive beyond at least one floral arrangement or plant is a place for cards. To securely manage these cards, which often contain cash, checks, and gift cards, consider creating or buying a wedding box that allows people to put in envelopes of most sizes but does not allow envelopes to be easily pulled out. Unless you're hiring someone to man this area all night, use the box or another secure plan to ensure that you can enjoy yourselves with ease till dawn—and later be able to enjoy those generous gifts from your loved ones.

THE CAKE TABLE • Though it may be the sweet finale of the evening, your wedding cake is likely to be on display earlier in the reception. Treat it like the star that it is with an extra layer of sumptuous linens or, for an elegant style, maybe tall silver candlesticks with tapered candles.

THE BAR • Bars at weddings tend to draw a crowd. Whether it's a venue-provided bar or one you're bringing in, estimate how much of it will be available for decorations, such as signs explaining the meanings behind a signature drink or the classic admonition: EAT, DRINK, AND BE MARRIED! If you're ordering personalized wedding cocktail napkins, consult with your caterer on how many you might need for the bar area.

THE DESSERT STATION • Parting is such sweet sorrow, which is why some couples offer a candy and dessert station for the end of the evening. Work with your caterer or figure out DIY ways to make this station pop with pizazz for more visual impact in the room. If the desserts are portable, use signage to encourage guests to take some home. Provide take-home containers.

THE COFFEE STATION • If your budget allows, you can also customize the coffee station with monogrammed coffee stirrers, napkins, and compostable coffee cups.

THE GUEST TABLES • We reviewed various dining table arrangements on page 118, and we'll go over centerpiece options on page 157. But decorating them is essential for the ocular pleasure alone. Work with your florist and catering team to bring your vision to life—and hear them out on their ideas too. Here are a few thoughts to get you started:

- **Add a sprig of herbs**: Bring your love of the garden into the decor. For a fragrant touch, add herbs like rosemary or lavender to the place settings. All the details matter when you want to wow.
- **Rent colored glassware**: Make your tables pop with colored glassware that falls within your wedding color palette. Think you can't afford it? Cut back on something else in your reception budget.
- **Source a pattern to run the table**: Stir things up with a modern patterned table runner and ditch the big floral centerpieces. Add smaller bud vases and rented china.
- **Rethink your table numbers**: Want something original for your table labels? Think about number presentation. Display your table numbers or names on unique vessels like wine bottles, lanterns, moss topiaries, or faux library books.

THE KIDS' TABLE • Want your pint-sized guests to have their own fun at your wedding and enjoy the reception? See if the caterer can lower their table and bring in a smaller set of chairs. Also, nix the linen and bring in heavy-duty rolled paper for the table covering so the artists can get straight to work between nibbles. Put out small jelly jars of monochromatic groupings of crayons and kid-friendly bags of tricks, such as plastic rings, glow sticks, and micro bottles of bubbles.

WEDDING FAVORS

The best ways to ensure that every guest gets their favors is to incorporate smaller favors into the design of each table setting and to deliver larger favors to your guests' rooms during the reception, if your reception is part of a hotel or resort.

LOOK UP! ABOVE THE RECEPTION

DRAPE THE CEILINGS • It's amazing what fabric draped around rafters or the ceiling can do. Keep it formal and luxurious with white fabric, or if you're seeking a fun vibe, opt for a bright color like hot pink or orange. Bonus: going this route enables you to go lighter on the table decor and still get the same decked-out reception look.

BLOOMS IN THE AIR • Flowers don't have to be on your tables—they can go above them too! Suspending lush arrangements a few feet above your guests' dinner plates is a fun way to create a more intimate space—doing it around chandeliers can be especially romantic for intimate seated-dinner receptions.

SOMETHING'S AFOOT

THERE'S MORE ON THE DANCE FLOOR • Now more than ever before, the flooring of wedding receptions is getting its own attention. Floor designers create intricate patterns to delight and enchant anyone who looks down through artistic arrangements of colored tape, vinyl logos, or other designs, patterns, and shapes made possible because of lights above. Dance floors and other walkable areas can also feature unexpected elements such as LED light panels, mirrors, grass, wood, glass, and a mixture of mediums to create fun patterns.

SIGNS AND OTHER RECEPTION AREA DETAILS

MAMMOTH MONOGRAMS • Large monogrammed signs made of galvanized metal and lightbulbs, flowers and wire, balloons, ice sculptures, or carved wood are beautiful for photos and look amazing behind food stations. And let's face it—this is the only time in your life when such self-indulgence is celebrated!

LOVE SIGNS • Handwritten signs with a personalized message or quote are pure fun—and also a delightful way to decorate an entrance or jazz up the cocktail bar. Buy a unique framed mirror from a thrift store and spray paint the frame to match the rest of your decor. Drape the mirror with greenery or a flower garland and use metallic paint for the lettering.

PATTERNED PILLOWS • It's lovely to have some lounge areas in the reception space, and you can rent some pieces to furnish it. Head to a housewares department for pillows and cover them with your favorite patterned fabric for a few low-maintenance pops of festive color and pattern.

PHOTOS
The Photo Booth • If you're springing for a photo booth, trick it out with wacky and bizarre props from your own shopping spree at the party supply store or go full rental with a photo booth company and don't worry about the cleanup.

A Family Photo Wall • For an easy conversation starter, create a wall of family wedding photos. Devote a row to each of your families or mix them all up.

Photo Backdrops • Get creative and provide a focal point in the room that will double as a photo backdrop, such as natural or artistic layers of colors and shapes to capture guests' attention. These can be DIY or set up by your events team, such as giant paper flowers, garlands of greenery, succulents attached to the wall, gold tassels, balloons, chalkboard signs, flower walls, and more.

Tasks to Tackle

- Consider all ceremony decor items, including:
  - Aisle(s)
  - Altar
  - Audio
  - Backdrop
  - Ceremony space
  - Chuppah or arch
  - Family seating
  - Lighting
  - Parking signage
  - Ritual tables
  - Seating
  - Weather considerations
  - Welcome drink station
  - Welcome sign

- Consider all cocktail hour decor items, including:
  - Bar
  - DJ/band/ musician station
  - Escort table/wall
  - Furniture extras
  - Serving trays
  - Tables
  - Welcome sign

- Consider all reception decor items, including:
  - Beverage stations
  - Cake table
  - Dance floor
  - Dessert station
  - Dining tables
  - DJ table or soundstage
  - Escort card display
  - Food stations
  - Gift table
  - Guest book table
  - Kids' table
  - Lighting
  - Photo backdrops
  - Photo booth
  - Server trays
  - Tables
  - Wedding favors

CHAPTER SIXTEEN

FLOWERS

With your decor established, it's a perfect time to start thinking about additional details, such as florals and greenery. Love is blooming, and your floral arrangements will showcase your personality as a couple, fitting in with the theme and style you've chosen for your wedding. Follow this field guide to popular and lesser-known wedding flowers, important elements to consider for two bouquets or two boutonnieres, and a spotlight on flowers and plants for a more masculine wedding.

For some of you, we've now come to your favorite chapter. Maybe you even turned here first! For those of us who adore flowers, it's an intense honor to carry them, to wear them, and to decorate our wedding spaces with them. Even if you're not quite that enthralled with florals, you can still use them to adorn everything from your altar or chuppah at your ceremony to the centerpieces on your reception tables. The other decorations you select for your day—the banners, escort cards, signs, and so forth—will ideally complement the flowers and plants you've chosen so that everything blends together into one cohesive aesthetic display.

FLOWER POWER

If you're having small children—or even full-grown adults—as your flower petal tossers, don't forget to fill their baskets. If instead your aisle is being decorated with petals by your florist, you can have your flower attendants carry pomander balls, which are spheres covered in flowers and held by a looped ribbon.

If you wish to honor other people in your wedding, giving them flowers to wear or carry is a great way to do so. This is a meaningful option but not necessary; it can be decided on a case-by-case basis. You might want to provide wearable flowers for:

- Ceremony readers
- Extended family members (or those who love you as family)
- Guest book managers
- Officiant
- Ring bearer
- Siblings not acting as attendants
- Ushers

BOUTONNIERES

Boutonnieres are more than just an afterthought, especially for a wedding of two people wearing these small punches of personality. Bouts are traditionally worn by any person getting married who wishes to wear one, as well as by any attendants who wish to wear one. They can add color and texture to the lapels of a suit, creating a dashing look, but more significantly, they indicate the importance of the wearer.

If one of you is wearing a boutonniere and the other is carrying a bouquet, work with your florist so that they complement one another. If you're both wearing boutonnieres, consider whether you'd like to wear matching ones. If you're already matching your attire, you could change it up here in the stems or leaves you choose for the boutonniere, or even the ribbon tying it all together.

Your boutonnieres are typically delivered to the ceremony site before the wedding begins, but delivery can also depend on where you're getting dressed. Plan the delivery with your florist ahead of time, especially if you need for them to go to separate places where a variety of people—including your partner—are all getting ready.

News Flash: You Don't Need Wedding Flowers

If anyone's pressuring you to think otherwise, it has now been written in a wedding book that you are not required to have one single stem at your wedding. Any item in the world can serve as a stand-in for flowers. Plants and succulents. Candy. Antiques. Ceramics. Art. Rattan balls. Ribbons. Nautical tchotchkes you picked up at a home goods store or during your world travels. Try succulents, tropical greenery, dusty miller, clover, herbs, olive leaves, eucalyptus stems with berries, or snowberries. Bonsai trees. Lego structures if you're young at heart. Woodland topiaries. An homage to your favorite Hollywood films if you're movie buffs, or foreign countries if you're travelers. It's okay to decorate your wedding with whatever you and your event designer can imagine. Let your heart go wild. As long as there's consistency and someone on your team to help you get it all to the space, you can pull it off.

Typically, your florist would be able to send only one staff member to one off-location boutonniere drop-off before getting to your wedding site to set up.

You might not want any flowers for your boutonniere. The right florist can help you find what's right for you—maybe a succulent or something completely different. But you'll need to speak up. Tell the florist what you like, but also what you don't like. If you like a preppy look, say so. If you're into goth, tell the florist—they might have just the plan for you with deep reds and blackish-blue petals. Alternatives to fluffy roses that are still in the floral family include thin freesia and aster. Or perhaps you'd like a gentleman's antique stickpin plus a feather and a ribbon.

Even though "boutonniere" is French for "buttonhole," don't mistakenly stick yours there. Boutonnieres should be discreetly attached to the left lapel at the top of the buttonhole, stem down but visible.

BOUQUETS

Ordering your bouquet—whether it's one or two—can be a thrilling moment in the wedding planning process. It's romantic, it's elegant, and it's practical, as it gives you somewhere to put your hands when you're feeling all kinds of emotions on your big day.

There are a variety of bouquets, all with their own names and characteristics. Your bouquet helps convey the style of your wedding—no matter what that style is, there is a type of bouquet that is perfect for it.

Are you drawn to drama, with an affinity for glitz and glamour, or does a love of nature and minimalism define you? There's a bouquet to fit each person searching for one; it's just about finding the right bundle of blooms to suit you.

So what should your bouquet look like? It's a good idea to match it to your body size to some extent. A minuscule nosegay might get lost held in front of a tall and voluptuous body, and a floral waterfall cascading down a shorter body might drown out that smaller frame.

UNDERSTANDING STEM COST • Wedding flowers can come with a hefty price tag, not only because of the type of flowers involved but also because providing wedding flowers is a labor-intensive process for the florist. Weddings (versus other special events) typically involve more meetings, deliveries of flowers to multiple places, more task-intensive install and takedown, and sometimes overly needy customers.

Follow these tips for cutting down your wedding flower costs:

1. Choose flowers that are in season in your region. Using local blooms cuts down on travel cost, and the price decreases significantly for in-season flowers.

2. Be open to substituting similar flowers if the flowers you want aren't in premium condition when you're making the arrangements.

3. Allow your blooms and buds to be repurposed. Transferring the ceremony decor to the reception can shave off costs.

4. Choose large flowers, such as hydrangeas, to take up more space.

5. Swap out some flowers for greenery, such as ferns or dusty miller, which is far cheaper.

BOUQUET STYLES • Understanding what's available to you will help you envision what best reflects your style.

- **Arm or presentation**: This is a Miss America–style of carrying long-stemmed flowers in the crook of the arm.
- **Breakaway**: This bouquet comes apart to form separate bouquets, one for tossing and others for giving away to mothers, attendants, and close friends.
- **Cascade**: This is the bouquet for anyone looking to make a major style statement. Cascading bouquets are all about the drama of florals spilling over the carrier's hands, creating the effect of a waterfall of blooming buds, plants, and/or ivy. Cascade bouquets are often carried in an out-of-sight holder.
- **Collar**: The outermost ring of the bouquet, the collar can be made of flowers, leaves, fabric, or feathers.

On equallywed.com, we've featured cisgender gay men wearing suits and capes and carrying bouquets, lesbians in masculine suits carrying bouquets, gender-nonconforming queer men carrying bouquets, and femme queer cis and trans women self-identified as brides carrying bouquets. Today there is no one type of person who's allowed to enjoy carrying a bouquet. There's no bouquet law. If you enjoy it, do it. If you don't enjoy it, don't do it. That's the tradition of LGBTQ+ weddings.

- **Composite:** Truly a work of art, the composite bouquet is made from hundreds of real flower petals wired together to essentially create one giant flower. Unique, out-of-the-box, and typically more expensive, this bouquet is a stunner.

- **Cuff:** The cuff is the ribbon, fabric, or leaves that hold together the stems of a bouquet. Sometimes the cuff is personalized with jewelry, charms, embroidery, or other embellishments.

- **Hand-tied:** If you're going for a more casual feel, this may be the way to go. Put simply, it's a bundle of flowers gathered and hand-tied with ribbon or burlap. The stems are left exposed so that the bouquet looks less stiff and formal.

- **Nosegay:** Nosegay bouquets are smaller (eighteen inches in diameter) and circular and can be held in one hand. They often incorporate more leafy greenery and other natural elements with tightly wrapped stems. A type of nosegay sometimes referred to as a tussie-mussie is even smaller and can fit into a conical silver holder. In a tradition passed down from the Victorian era, honored people in the couple's circle sometimes carry these.

How to Carry a Bouquet

Carrying a bouquet like a pro is not an innate skill. It takes practice. Unless you're carrying an arm bouquet, the bouquet should be at about the same area as your belly button (not in front of your chest and not below the waist). Keep it several inches away from your body, as the pollen from the flowers could rub onto your wedding attire or your petals could get crushed. Practice walking with something similar at home—or even just with your hands held together. You might even be gifted with a faux bouquet of ribbons from your presents at a wedding shower (bring it to your rehearsal!). Have all your attendants who are carrying bouquets practice as well.

- **Posy:** The exact opposite of the cascading bouquet would probably be the posy bouquet. Delicate and understated, this bouquet can be carried in one hand and often is adorned with ribbon.
- **Sheath:** A sheath is a handful of long-stemmed flowers held in the crook of the arm and tied together in a ribbon. It's much like the arm or presentation bouquet, but simpler and has fewer flowers.
- **Toss:** This is a slimmed-down version of your heavier bouquet whose sole purpose is to be tossed. Photo op! See if your florist will add long ribbons (love knots) in your wedding colors for even prettier photos when you throw it into the air.
- **Wired:** Unlike a hand-tied bouquet, a wired bouquet has wires inserted into each stem or taped to the flowers to create a particular silhouette or make the flowers work in an arrangement.

. . .

Favorite Wedding Florals

The following list of the flowers most commonly used in weddings includes the season they're most likely to be available, their meaning, and the available shades.

ACACIA (MIMOSA)
Season: Late winter, spring
Meaning: Purity, immortality, or hidden love
Shade: Bright yellow

AGAPANTHUS
Season: Spring, summer
Meaning: Good weather, love, or patience
Shades: Blue, white, violet-blue

AMARYLLIS
Season: Naturally spring, but can be propagated anytime
Meaning: Determination, passionate desire, or radiant beauty
Shades: Red, pink, white, lavender, variegated

ANEMONE
Season: Spring, summer, or fall
Meaning: Anticipation and undying love
Shades: White, red, blue, pale yellow, purple

APPLE BLOSSOM
Season: Spring, summer
Meaning: Good fortune, health, and youth
Shades: White, light pink, pink

ASIATIC LILIES
Season: Summer, but can be propagated anytime
Meaning: Flirtatiousness, innocence, and beauty
Shades: White, yellow, peach, pink, orange, red, variegated

ASTER
Season: Summer, fall
Meaning: Love, gentleness, and hope
Shades: Light blue, blue, purple, pink, white

BABY'S BREATH
Season: Late spring, summer, fall
Meaning: Purity of heart
Shade: White

BACHELOR'S BUTTON (CORNFLOWER)
Season: Spring, summer
Meaning: Bravery, blessings, or felicity
Shades: Usually bright blue or violet-blue; also white, pink, dark
    maroon (black)

BELLS OF IRELAND
Season: Summer
Meaning: Luck, fanciful hopes, or tranquillity
Shades: Light green to green

BIRD OF PARADISE
Season: Fall, winter
Meaning: Joy and faithfulness
Shades: Yellow, orange, red

CALLA LILY
Season: Spring, summer (but like many other bulbs, can be brought to
    bloom at any time)
Meaning: Magnificent beauty, marriage, or transformation and rebirth
Shades: White, green, pink, yellow, orange, purple

CAMELLIA
Season: Fall, winter
Meaning: Longing, adoration, or devotion (Chinese)
Shades: Pink, red, white, lavender, variegated

CARNATION

Season: Any

Meaning: Fascination, love, yearning, admiration, health, and energy

Shades: Pink, red, white, yellow, purple, orange, peach, green, variegated

CASABLANCA LILY

Season: Spring

Meaning: Celebration

Shades: White, cream, yellow

CHEROKEE ROSE

Season: Fall, winter

Meaning: Love, beauty, desire, hope, and regeneration

Shades: White, light pink, pink

CHRYSANTHEMUM

Season: Any

Meaning: Happiness, honesty, and encouragement (Japan)

Shades: White, yellow, pink, green, orange, red

COSMOS

Season: Spring, fall

Meaning: Balance and peace

Shades: White, pink, orange, yellow, red

CRASPEDIA (BILLY BALLS OR BILLY BUTTONS)

Season: Spring, summer

Meaning: Happiness, joyful, playfulness

Shade: Yellow

DAHLIA

Season: Summer, fall

Meaning: Dignity, elegance, and good taste

Shades: Yellow, white, pink, orange, lavender, variegated

DAISY

Season: Late spring, summer

Meaning: Innocence, loyalty, new beginnings

Shades: White, lavender, pink around a yellow disk

DELPHINIUM
Season: Spring, summer
Meaning: Heavenly, beautiful spirit, or lightness
Shades: Blue, purple, white

DUSTY MILLER
Season: Any
Meaning: Calmness
Shade: Silver (foliage)

ESKIMO ROSE
Season: Late summer, fall, winter
Meaning: Purity or reverence
Shades: White, ivory

FORGET-ME-NOT
Season: Spring
Meaning: True love, memories, unflinching devotion
Shade: Bright blue

FORSYTHIA
Season: Spring
Meaning: Anticipation and hope
Shade: Yellow

FREESIA
Season: Spring
Meaning: Trust, innocence, closeness
Shades: White, lavender, purple, yellow, pink, orange, red

GARDENIA
Season: Spring, summer
Meaning: Beauty, admiration, good luck, and hidden love
Shades: Cream, white

GERBER DAISY
Season: Fall, winter
Meaning: Strength, purity, beauty, and cheerfulness
Shades: Pink, red, yellow, white, orange, peach, salmon

GLOXINIA
Season: Late spring, summer
Meaning: Love at first sight
Shades: Purple, lavender, white, maroon

HEATHER
Season: Late summer, fall
Meaning: Protection, granted wishes, guidance
Shades: Purple, mauve, white, pink, lavender, magenta, red, copper, silver, green

HELIOTROPE
Season: Spring, summer, or fall, depending on the climate
Meaning: Search for truth, honor, hope, or devotion
Shades: Purple, lavender, white, blue, mauve

HIBISCUS
Season: Spring through fall (or any season in a warm climate)
Meaning: Desire, love, feminine power, or delicate beauty (Hawaii)
Shades: Pink, lavender, red, yellow, white, blue, peach, orange, variegated

HOLLY
Season: Winter (berries)
Meaning: Domestic bliss or protection
Shades: Red (berries), green (foliage), white (flowers)

HYACINTH (SEE ALSO MUSCARI)
Season: Spring
Meaning: Playfulness, constancy, and sincere affection
Shades: Purple, red, blue, orange, white, pink, mauve, yellow

HYDRANGEA
Season: Summer
Meaning: Understanding, enlightenment, or unabashed love
Shades: Blue, pink, green, red, lavender, yellow, maroon, white, variegated

IRIS
Season: Summer
Meaning: Wisdom, devotion or strength, vitality, and boldness
Shades: White, yellow, pink, magenta, blue, purple, variegated

JASMINE
Season: Spring, summer
Meaning: Love, vision, and affluence
Shades: White, light yellow, golden

LAVENDER
Season: Summer
Meaning: Romance, peace, or LGBTQ+
Shades: Purple, light purple, blue

LILAC
Season: Spring
Meaning: First love (purple) or youthfulness (white)
Shades: Purple, white, light pink

LILY OF THE VALLEY
Season: Spring
Meaning: Sweetness, a return to happiness or fulfillment
Shade: White

LISIANTHUS
Season: Summer
Meaning: Heartfelt desire, boldness, and communication
Shades: White, pink, lavender, deep purple, bicolors (like violet-blue)

MARIGOLD
Season: Summer, fall, and sometimes winter
Meaning: Passion, creativity, harmony, truth, and good cheer
Shades: Yellow, orange, red, rusty red, bicolored

MODERN GARDEN ROSE
Season: Primarily spring and fall, but available continuously throughout the year
Meaning (varies with color): Love, sensuality, passion, or immortal union
Shades: Cream, white, peach, coral, red, maroon, pink, lavender, yellow, bicolor, or even brown

MUSCARI (GRAPE HYACINTH)
Season: Spring
Meaning: Forgiveness, loveliness, or lasting love
Shades: Light and dark blue contrast, cobalt blue, white, mauve

NARCISSUS (DAFFODILS, PAPERWHITES, JONQUILS)
Season: Winter, early spring
Meaning: Beauty, sweetness, or high self-esteem
Shades: Golden yellow, light yellow, white, or a contrast of these shades

ORCHID
Season: Fall, winter
Meaning: Love, beauty, refinement, maturity, or fertility
Shades: Pink, lavender, purple, red, orange, yellow, salmon, variegated, white

PANSY
Season: Early spring and summer; fall and winter in warm climates
Meaning: Merriment, deep love, or thoughtfulness
Shades: Blue, yellow, red, orange, copper, bronze, lavender, purple, white, mixed

PARROT TULIP
Season: Late spring, summer
Meaning: Light, hope, beauty, or avowed love
Shades: Peach, red, white, orange, yellow, pink, mauve, lavender, black, rainbow (these are frequently variegated)

PEONY
Season: Spring
Meaning: Happiness, desire, wedded bliss, or prosperity
Shades: Pink, light pink, white, lavender, purple, magenta, blue

POINSETTIA
Season: Fall, winter
Meaning: Purity, beauty, hope, or celebration
Shades: Red, light green, white, pink, variegated (foliage)

POPPY
Season: Spring, summer
Meaning: Pleasure, imagination, rejuvenation, or eternal life
Shades: Gold, yellow, orange, red, blue, lavender, pink

QUEEN ANNE'S LACE
Season: Fall, winter
Meaning: Sanctuary, grace, or elegance
Shades: White, ivory, pink, light purple

RANUNCULUS
Season: Spring, early summer
Meaning: Radiance, beauty, or fascination
Shades: White, yellow-gold, peach, bronze, orange, deep red,
bright green, pink, hot pink

ROSE
Season: Any, but easiest to find in spring and fall
Meaning: Beauty, beginnings, desire, unity, and eternal love
Shades: Bright red, deep red, pink, white, cream, orange, yellow,
mauve, lavender

SNOWBERRY
Season: Fall, winter
Meaning: Destined or fated
Shades: White, light pink (fruit)

SUNFLOWER
Season: Late summer, fall
Meaning: Pure thoughts, longevity, or happiness
Shades: Yellow, gold around a darker center

SWEET PEA
Season: Late spring, early summer
Meaning: Bliss, departure, adventure, or fresh starts
Shades: Purple, bright pink, white, blue, lavender, mauve, variegated, mixed

SWEET WILLIAM
Season: Summer
Meaning: Gallantry or cheer
Shades: Pink, lavender, white, deep red, variegated

TULIP
Season: Late winter, spring
Meaning: Passion, perfect love
Shades: Red, yellow, pink, purple, orange, maroon, white, salmon, lavender, deep purple, mixed

VIOLET
Season: Late winter, spring, year-round
Meaning: Modesty, faithfulness, affection, or taking chances (white)
Shades: Periwinkle, purple, blue, lavender, pink, mauve, white

WISTERIA
Season: Spring, summer
Meaning: Closeness, affection, and spontaneity
Shades: Lavender, purple

ZINNIA
Season: Late spring, summer, early fall
Meaning: Lasting affection, constancy, or goodness
Shades: Orange, purple, red, golden yellow, pale yellow, green, white, variegated

Preserving Flowers

The tried-and-true DIY method of preserving flowers is to keep your bouquet's thirst quenched by placing it in a vase after your ceremony and photos are over. Assign a trusted friend to get it home safely and in the refrigerator for you. Afterward, you can freeze-dry your bouquet or boutonniere, and then display it in your home for as long as there's color in it. After the color fades, dry out your bouquet or bout by hanging the stems separately upside down. You can even make potpourri from the buds.

Professional services are available for preserving your bouquet or boutonniere under a glass dome, but you might end up having to have another bouquet made for that purpose if yours is looking limp or parched. Perhaps it's better to save that money and celebrate your one-year anniversary with a floral arrangement that resembles your bouquet or boutonniere, or a combination of the two if you both carried or wore one.

A CASE FOR ORGANIC FLOWERS

If cutting down on the amount of pesticides you're exposed to in terms of the food you consume is important to you, consider organic flowers for your wedding. The flower industry is nearly dependent on chemical-laden blooms coated in nearly fifty times the fungicides and pesticides used on food. This puts not only you at risk, but also flower farmers, many of whom have suffered from miscarriages, vision problems, and other health issues as a direct result of these chemicals. Sourcing certified organic flowers for your wedding may very well increase your cost per stem, but the conscious act is safer for you, your attendants, and your guests, as well as the ones who do the hard work growing, harvesting, and working with the gorgeous flowers before you even see them.

ATTENDANT BOUQUETS

Although the attendants' bouquets should be smaller than the marriers' bouquet(s), their bouquets should resemble the main bouquets in color, shape, and type of flower. They also should complement the attire. Also, just as a reminder, you should pay for your attendants' bouquets.

QUESTIONS TO ASK WHEN HIRING A FLORIST

- Have you ever worked with an LGBTQ+ couple before? *Of course you'll want your vendors to ask about who's wearing or carrying what kind of personal flowers, but in a supportive way, not a demeaning way. Awkward jokes here can be ugly and downright hurtful. What is helpful is a florist who uses inclusive language, who generally understands gender fluidity, and who can ensure that each person, from the couple to the chosen family to the attendants, will be wearing or carrying an arrangement that best honors who they are.*

- Are the flowers I want in season? *If you're not prepared to pay more for out-of-season flowers, be open to cheaper alternatives.*

- Where do you source your flowers from? *If it's important to you that the flowers be ethically sourced and organic, but the florist doesn't mention it, be sure to ask.*

- What's the price per stem?

- How many stems will be included in each floral arrangement? *Though some artistic license should be afforded the florist, you want to make sure that you're getting bouquets, boutonnieres, arrangements, and centerpieces that are the size you want.*

- How will my order be delivered? *Most florists or their staff will come to the venue to set everything up themselves. If you're not getting ready at the venue, make sure you know when your personal flowers will be delivered to you. Freshly delivered flowers make for great photos while you're dressing and primping.*

- Will you package all your supplies up when the wedding is over and take them with you?

- If you need to substitute flowers at the last minute based on availability, will I have a say in color and look?

Tasks to Tackle

- Explore flowers that you love and create a portfolio of them, either digitally or in a notebook, to show to your florist.

- Talk with your attendants about the flowers you'd like them to wear or carry and make sure they're comfortable with the plan and how it aligns with their gender expression.

- Practice carrying a bouquet and/or pinning a boutonniere.

- Make final decisions about flowers and where you'll need them.

- Schedule a final meeting with your florist.

Part Three

ESSENTIAL DETAILS

CHAPTER SEVENTEEN

PARTIES

Surrounding your big event are soirees to celebrate every part of the fact that you're tying the knot. Some parties you can host, while others can be thrown in your honor. Each one has its own purpose, traditions, and etiquette guidelines. Let's delve into all the ways to celebrate your love!

THE ENGAGEMENT PARTY

The engagement party is typically thrown in your honor after your engagement is announced. Traditionally, parents or close friends of the couple host this event, but the host could be anyone who has the means and interest. Follow the etiquette rule and work with your host to keep the guest list limited to only the people you are certain you'll be inviting to the wedding. Some guests may bring gifts to the engagement party, but they are not to be expected, nor should you share registry information for this purpose. The engagement party is strictly about celebrating the happy couple. The venue could be a restaurant, your home, a neighborhood bar, a rented room in any number of venues, or an event space, such as a hotel terrace.

WEDDING SHOWERS

The original purpose of the wedding shower was to help the couple prepare for life after marriage in a combined household—the assumption being that they were not living together before their wedding. Today the gifts and purpose have shifted in light of the modern understanding that couples usually live together before marriage (gasp!), but the spirit of wanting to provide for the couple remains. Thus, the couple is showered with gifts as a way of imparting blessings on them and happy wishes. Even though you and your spouse-to-be might already be living together, new items you will love are certain to be a welcome addition to your household.

Wedding showers have historically been held with each betrothed person, their own attendants, and their part of the guest list who might have a similar gender expression. But friendships don't always work that way—does your best friend have a different gender identity from you, but you want your friend at all the parties? Then do it! Wedding showers are your chance to be showered with love by your closest friends.

Anyone can throw the engaged couple a wedding shower, but typically the main shower for each person is planned and executed by the honor attendants. Although it used to be considered poor form for a close family member to host your wedding shower because of the implication that you yourself were essentially asking for gifts, today the floor is open to anyone wishing to host.

If multiple people want to throw you a wedding shower, consider yourself blessed. But also consider the guests at those showers. Is there crossover in the guest list from shower to shower? Guests spend an average of $700 on weddings, doling out cash for presents, outfits, travel, gas, and sometimes airfare and lodging. Typically showers are spread out among different groups—such as coworkers, neighborhood friends, childhood friends, your current social circle, and your parent's friends—to reduce the chance of crossover. If it does seem like one or more people are being invited to multiple showers, don't exclude them from future events—they might wonder what they've done to slight you—but ask the host to tell them not to bring a gift but to come only for the fellowship. It's better to have someone else convey your wishes because, coming from you, that message might imply that you're focusing on the gifts, not the person.

If multiple people in the same social circle want to throw a shower for you and there's a significant amount of guest-list crossover, you might suggest that they get together on a single shower so that your guests don't feel compelled to attend them all.

Some couples choose to forgo their individual showers and to have a combined couple's shower with all of their wedding guests who live nearby. This can be fun, but it also doubles the guest count for the one event (thus doubling the cost), so be even more gracious to your hosts and make sure that they're getting the support they need to throw this party for you.

SHOWER GIFTS • Shower gifts are typically smaller and less expensive supplements to wedding presents. Almost anything the couple can use is appropriate, but the host can designate a specific gift category on the invitation. If you have a preference, tell your host early in the shower planning. The host can also mention on the shower invitations the particular group of gift types you may have registered for and suggest that guests buy something within that category. Shower hosts want to make you happy, and they'll probably ask you what kind of shower you'd like to have and what best meets your needs. The following ideas about gift category choices will prime your thinking about what kind of shower you'd like to have:

- Bar: Social drinkers love the bar-themed shower, especially when it's held in the evening and cocktails are served during the party. Make sure to register for popular bar gifts like shakers, jiggers, muddlers, strainers, bar spoons, flasks, chillers, fine liqueurs and cordials, a make-your-own beer kit, specialty bitters and shrubs, liquor, wine, decanters, wine openers, wineglasses, cocktail glasses, beer glasses, and bar decor.
- Game room: A game room theme is excellent for couples who enjoy game nights with family and friends. Suggested gifts include playing cards, poker chips, indoor sports equipment, board games, and personalized gifts.
- Kitchen: Whether you're a culinary genius or a kitchen novice, the

wedding shower can be an opportunity to expand or upgrade your epicurean tools, from pots, pans, and cooking utensils to small appliances, baking dishes, canisters, and gadgets.

- **Library**: Lovers of literature will appreciate this shower theme most of all. Gift suggestions include current best sellers, classic works, books of sonnets and love poems, cookbooks, reading lamps, bookends, a dictionary, magazine subscriptions, and books about gardening, birding, and home improvement.
- **Lingerie**: Lingerie showers work best with smaller gatherings of only your closest friends.
- **Recipes**: Guests bring a favorite recipe along with some of the ingredients and/or the container in which it is prepared or served. For example, a cake recipe might come with a sack of flour and a sifter, or a colander and a box of noodles might complement a pasta recipe. The host provides uniform recipe cards and a box to contain all the recipes brought by guests.

Make sure that you have registered for enough items to accommodate the number of showers thrown in your honor—and at multiple price points. Shower gifts tend to be less expensive than wedding gifts.

Traditionally toward the middle to the end of the shower, all the guests gather around to watch you open the gifts, attentively oohing and aahing over each item. If it's not a couple's shower, attendants and close friends sometimes sneak some wedding-night surprises into the gifts, making it all the more convivial. Ask someone to stay nearby taking notes on who gave what, so you'll be able to send timely thank-you notes. It's easy to get caught up in the excitement of opening presents and then wonder, once most people have left, which tea towel set or chef's knife goes with which gift tag.

After all the gifts have been opened at your shower, and while you still have everyone's attention, stand up and thank everyone for coming and for their generosity. Direct some extra special consideration toward your host or hosts, expressing your gratitude for their friendship and for all the work and time they spent on the wonderful shower.

CHARMING CONFECTIONS • If you're having a small wedding, consider adding the custom of baking gold or silver charms, each with a special meaning, into a cake served for dessert at the shower. Be sure to instruct your guests to pull on the attached ribbon to take the charm out before they bite into the cake. Each charm will bring its recipient a different kind of special luck:

- **Heart**: True love
- **Ring**: Upcoming engagement
- **Clover, shamrock, or horseshoe**: Luck
- **Flower**: Growing love
- **Wishing well**: Wishes granted
- **Anchor, airplane, or ship's wheel**: Travel and adventure
- **High chair or baby carriage**: Children
- **Rocking chair**: Long life
- **Coin purse or money bag**: Good fortune
- **Wedding bells**: Upcoming marriage
- **Phone**: Good news
- **Picture frame**: Happy life

SHOWER GAMES • Games for wedding showers run the gamut from sweet and innocent to sexier games that used to be reserved for bach parties. As long as you are feeling safe and not having your values compromised, try to go along with any shower themes and games your hosts come up with. Be a good sport, put your best smile on, and be gracious. They're excited to be able to offer you their very best, and it is usually with the purest of intentions and the fullest of hearts. Honor this as best as you can.

HOST GIFT • At each shower hosted in your honor, you'll need a complete list of who was involved in throwing it. Their generous gift of throwing you a shower should be acknowledged with your gift to them; a simple thank-you note is not enough. Your present to the host doesn't need to be expensive but can be a personalized expression of gratitude, such as beribboned vases of flowers from your garden, jars of your world-famous pepper jelly, sets of monogrammed stationery for each host—whatever feels right coming from you.

BACH PARTIES

Known as "the fling before the ring," bach (a shortened, gender-neutral use of bachelor or bachelorette) parties are wildly different from wedding showers. First and foremost, the entire mission of this party is to let the last waves of freedom wash over you before you are officially committed to your sweetheart for the rest of your days. Don't panic. That carefree feeling will be with you in your marriage too. But it's different when you're officially married.

Although you don't need to be any particular gender to get married, gendered terms are all too frequently used for all things wedding, and especially around bach events. If you'd like to de-gender the terms "bachelor" and "bachelorette," consider these clever alternatives:

- Bach bash
- Bach party
- Best night ever
- Buck party
- Friendship fete
- Hen party
- Stag party
- The fling before the ring

Sometimes the bach parties last longer than just one night. They can be elaborate weekend trips to faraway destinations. Your attendants typically arrange everything, including having all the guests pitch in to cover your costs. They should ask you what activities might be too far outside of your comfort zone, as well as work with you to come up with the guest list. (Make sure all guests also are invited to the wedding.) For this event, it's best to invite only your very closest friends.

Destinations for bach parties vary widely, from a beach house, cabin, or lake house rental for a week or a weekend to a jaunt across the globe for any number of ways to satisfy wanderlust; from a spa weekend, trip to Las Vegas, or pool party to a crazy night in a club; from attending a sporting event together to participating in a sport (sailing, golf, skiing, fishing) or taking a trip to a winery or craft brewery. Or any combination of the above.

BUDGET-FRIENDLY FRIEND GATHERINGS • With all of the other expenses your friends—and especially your attendants—are covering, sometimes it makes sense to have a more practical get-together. For daytime gatherings, DIY beauty and grooming parties provide bonding time along with serious pampering, a fun day hike costs hardly anything at all, and hitting up a festival in the park and enjoying free live music gives you a chance to cut loose and enjoy your friends. Having a potluck dinner, with each friend bringing a dish or a few bottles of good wine or beer, will cost less than a fancy restaurant would charge, you won't have to tip, and there'll be no time restriction on your evening together.

TIMELINE • Bach parties are best held about a month before the wedding, to give everyone involved time to budget both the time and money they'll be investing in traveling for your wedding. Also, there's a chance of a hangover from these parties, and you don't want that troll anywhere near your wedding day.

Some partners enjoy this time with their attendants without their spouse-to-be, while others feel more comfortable having a combined bach party. One fast-rising trend is for the two separate groups enjoying time to themselves, perhaps at separate dinners or their own daytime activities, to meet up sometime in the evening at a nightclub, a hookah bar, a karaoke bar, or a bowling alley.

ATTENDANT APPRECIATION PARTIES

Attendant appreciation parties are typically held one to two days before the wedding, either in one event with both of you and all of your attendants or in separate events with each of you and your respective attendants. Hosted by either marrier, the couple, or a close family member or friend, these parties typically offer a laid-back way to enjoy the wedding week even more. A classic attendant appreciation party is a day or evening meal, but nowadays fun alternatives include golf, spa time, a picnic in the park, a cocktail party, a day at the lake or beach, a short hike, or a sightseeing adventure in your city. These parties are an ideal time for bestowing gifts on your attendants, though some couples choose to present the gifts at the reception.

THE REHEARSAL DINNER

Typically held the night before the wedding, the rehearsal dinner is multifunctional. It feeds all the people who will have just been involved in rehearsing your wedding ceremony at your venue, and it's an opportunity to create a stronger bond between the two families who are now becoming one because of your marriage. The rehearsal dinner is customary, but certainly not mandatory.

WHO HOSTS? • If your parents are interested, one of them might volunteer to host this event, or another close family member could take on this responsibility, such as an uncle, aunt, or grandparent. If no one offers, then the couple is responsible for hosting the rehearsal dinner.

WHO IS INVITED? • Everyone who is required to be at the rehearsal—your wedding party, your officiant, your parents and siblings, everyone's respective children, and grandparents—should be invited. You are not expected to invite all out-of-town guests or the entire guest list from your wedding, but some couples do. The opportunity for intimacy might be lost, though, if you open the guest list up to more than the main players.

HOW IS EVERYONE INVITED? • Mailed invitations are preferred. This is a formal event, second only in importance to the wedding.

WHAT HAPPENS AT A REHEARSAL DINNER? • A welcoming event meant to encourage families and friends to get to know one another better before the big day, the rehearsal dinner might include toasts from the honor attendants, parents, and others honoring the couple, a slide show depicting the couple's love story, the couple bestowing individual gifts on their attendants (if they haven't already done so), and the couple giving presents to their parents.

WHERE IS THE REHEARSAL DINNER HELD? • There are no hard-and-fast rules for the rehearsal dinner venue. If you're employing technology in any way, such as a presenting a photo slide show, you might want a private room in the back of a restaurant. The rehearsal dinner is often held at a restaurant that is significant to you as a couple—perhaps it was one of your first date spots, or the restaurant serves a dish that you bonded over in another country and now you go there to remember that special feeling. But if another person or couple is hosting, they might choose somewhere that works for their own budget. If you dislike the place they've chosen, consider their reasons, and if you're still unhappy about it, determine what can be done about it before the invitations are mailed. Although you'd obviously like to be in on the decision-making process, keep in mind that your loved ones want to celebrate and honor you in their own way.

Depending on budget and imagination, rehearsal dinners can become quite elaborate, especially if linen rentals, catering, and floral design are involved. The dinner need not fit in with the theme of your wedding, as it is its own event, but it shouldn't outshine or compete with the wedding reception. If a formal seated dinner doesn't feel right to you, consider a clambake or a catered barbecue dinner on picnic tables at a local craft brewery.

HANDLING THE BILL • Even if your rehearsal dinner takes place at a restaurant or another venue where the bills normally appear on the table, make sure the tab is completely taken care of long before the end of the meal. It is the hosts' responsibility to cover all planned expenses for the rehearsal dinner. If you wish to keep costs down, offer guests only controlled choices of beer, wine, liquor, and certain pre-approved dishes. The best way to head off any hassles is to work with the restaurant to print menus specific to your event, thereby avoiding confusion and awkward moments—such as when your best friend orders the most expensive bourbon on the cocktail menu but your budget only allows for beer and wine. Out of sight, out of mind.

THE AFTER-PARTY

Keep the celebratory joy bouncing off the moon until the wee hours of the wedding night with an after-party. Nothing needs to be formalized beforehand, but if you want to make sure it happens, plan your after-party in advance by reserving a few tables at a club or your wedding hotel's late-night bar to guarantee that you'll have space for your crew. This is one party where everyone pays for themselves, though close friends typically take care of the newlyweds' tab. For more on the after-party, flip to page 109.

THE MORNING-AFTER BRUNCH

Held the morning after the wedding, the morning-after brunch serves as an official send-off for the couple before they depart on their honeymoon and gives them a chance to say thank you and good-bye to friends and family who have come from near and far to attend their wedding.

WHO HOSTS? • Anyone can host the morning-after brunch— parents, parental figures, grandparents, aunts, uncles, friends, even the couple themselves.

WHO IS INVITED? • All wedding guests are invited to the morning-after brunch. If the couple is taking off for their honeymoon the morning after their wedding, they might not attend. But everyone else still enjoys getting together and saying their good-byes.

HOW IS EVERYONE INVITED? • Because the morning-after brunch is informal, you can issue invitations with information about it in either printed or digital form, you can rely on word of mouth, or you can mention it on your wedding website. (Just remember that wedding websites are often public, so be considerate of the host's privacy if the brunch is held in a private residence.)

WHAT HAPPENS AT A MORNING-AFTER BRUNCH? • The morning-after brunch provides everyone with a chance for more hugs, for recalling fun stories from the wedding the night before, for wishing each other safe travels, for new friends to exchange contact information, and for sending everyone back to their regularly scheduled lives with warm hearts and full bellies.

WHERE IS THE MORNING-AFTER BRUNCH HELD? • Any venue will do. At hometown weddings with fewer than seventy-five guests, often a parent invites the wedding guests to stop by their home for a continental breakfast. For weddings in hotels or destination weddings, post-wedding brunches can be held on a private terrace, alongside a sparkling blue pool, or in a designated section of a restaurant.

ONE MORE THING • Guests will be leaving your wedding venue at various times, and some of them may not be able to stop by the brunch. Make it easy for those who can stop in by offering them coffee and a quick bite before they hit the road rather than an elaborate setup, which might discourage some guests with a plane to catch.

Tasks to Tackle

- Decide which parties you want to have.
- Create guest lists for all parties, even if someone else is hosting.
- Bring host gifts to showers.
- Practice speeches you might give at different parties.

ele

CHAPTER EIGHTEEN

MAKING IT LEGAL

It's a true victory that, as of June 26, 2015, marriage is now legally available to every American citizen. Now that our right to marriage has been recognized on both the state and federal levels, LGBTQ+ couples can add the exciting task of applying for the marriage license to their list of duties. If you're transgender but have not legally changed your gender identity as far as the government is concerned, you'll still have to follow the laws for same-sex marriage when applying for your marriage license.

HOW TO APPLY FOR A MARRIAGE LICENSE

DOMESTIC WEDDINGS • For a legally recognized marriage, the steps to getting married include applying for your marriage license before the wedding. Though guidelines differ from state to state, you'll generally need to visit the marriage bureau or city hall in the city and state where you'll be married at least three days prior to the wedding. There might be a waiting period, and you might have to have blood testing done prior to the issuance of the license. Therefore, it's critical that you do your homework on the requirements of your city and state one to two months before your wedding. Plan to provide identification and bring your checkbook, any required additional paperwork, and blood test results.

Keep in mind that most marriage licenses are valid only for a window of time—anywhere between ten days and a year—during which you must have the ceremony, sign the license (together with your officiant), and file for a certified license and marriage certificate.

DESTINATION WEDDINGS • When marrying abroad in another country, remember that many areas do not offer marriage equality for residents or visitors. Research ahead of time whether or not your wedding ceremony will be legally recognized in your venue's city. If it will, find out how to obtain a marriage license there and when you'll need to apply. Some resorts will handle the paperwork for you, but don't just leave it in their hands. Follow up as soon as you arrive to ensure that everything is handled properly. This is one item you don't want falling through the cracks.

Until we achieved full marriage equality in the United States, same-sex couples were often forced to travel to other states to legally marry and then hold their wedding ceremonies either in that state or back at home. It is still the norm that couples who are legally identified as the same gender need to legally marry in their home state either before or after their destination wedding ceremony.

If you're Americans having a destination wedding in the United States, find out what the laws are in your venue's county. You should easily be able to obtain a marriage license, but the waiting period, required paperwork, and fees vary from state to state, and sometimes county to county.

CHANGING YOUR NAME

If you, your partner, or both of you are changing your name, you don't need to go through the hoops that your predecessors did just a few years ago: petitioning the court for permission to take your spouse's last name, running an advertisement in the newspaper about your plans to change your name, and sometimes paying thousands in lawyer's fees. All that is behind us now, and today you can easily change your name following these steps:

CHOOSE YOUR NAME • Decide on your name change before you apply for your marriage license. The name you want to use once you're married is the one you'll write on the application.

GET YOUR MARRIAGE CERTIFICATE • Before you can change your name, you'll need the original certified marriage license with the raised seal and your new last name on it. Contact the clerk's office where your marriage license was filed to obtain copies if one wasn't automatically sent to you.

CHANGE YOUR SOCIAL SECURITY CARD • Go online to the Social Security Administration's website. Fill out the application for a new Social Security card with your new name. You'll keep the same number; only your name will change. Mail in your application or bring it and a certified copy of your marriage license to the local Social Security Administration office.

CHANGE YOUR DRIVER'S LICENSE • Once you've obtained your new Social Security card, visit the local Department of Motor Vehicles office to get a new license with your new last name. Check the website to confirm what identification your county requires, but plan to bring in your current driver's license, your certified marriage license, and your new Social Security card.

UPDATE YOUR BANK ACCOUNTS • Whether you're setting up a new joint account or updating your current accounts, bring your bank up to speed on your new name. Take your new driver's license and your certified marriage license to your local bank's branch to change the name attached to your accounts and to request new checks and debit and credit cards.

UPDATE ALL OTHER ACCOUNTS • Once you've obtained your new Social Security card and driver's license with your married name, you need to notify companies where you have accounts of your new legal name. For security reasons and to avoid the risk of identity fraud, some may require you to fax or mail in a copy of your certified marriage certificate; with others, you'll be able to get it taken care of with a phone call.

Places to Notify
- Attorney (to update legal documents, including your will)
- Credit card companies
- Doctors' offices
- Electric and other utility companies
- Employers/payroll
- Insurance companies (auto, home, life, health)
- Investment account providers
- Mortgage company or landlord
- Passport office
- Post office
- Schools and alumni associations
- Voter registration office

Tasks to Tackle

- Research marriage license requirements in the location where you're getting married.
- Bring your marriage license to the wedding.
- Sign your marriage license with your officiant on your wedding day.
- Notify everyone of your new name, if you're changing it.

CHAPTER NINETEEN

GIFTS

There's a pervasive rumor floating around that because some LGBTQ+ couples are getting married later in life, they don't need to register for gifts. Untrue! All couples deserve the opportunity to receive wedding gifts, whether they're starting out in life and could use some basic household items to build their happy nest, or they're established enough to be upgrading to finer china and higher-thread-count sheets. And keep in mind that registries can be set up not just for run-of-the-mill or traditional wedding presents but for more adventurous items! Many guests will also enjoy buying more exciting gifts, such as items for the garden or a microbrewery starter kit or experiences.

Wedding gifts used to be given to couples who were leaving their parents' homes and needed everything to set up their own household. Today most couples already have at least some of the basics, but wedding gifts still give guests a great opportunity to celebrate the couple with presents to use in their life together going forward.

Whether you're registering with a traditional store, using an online registry site, inviting guests to skip the registry, asking for cash for a honeymoon or a new house, or declining gifts altogether, it's critical to follow wedding gift etiquette by thoughtfully communicating your wishes to your guests, keeping track of all your gifts, and, above all else, graciously thanking each person with a handwritten note of appreciation.

GIFT REGISTRIES

The purpose of a gift registry is to give your guests options. It's a list of suggested purchases—preselected items or activities that you and your spouse-to-be would love to own or experience. But they really are just suggestions, and if you look at it this way, rather than as a shopping list you're handing out to a lot of people, you'll feel more delighted to receive any of the gifts and won't react as some couples do, which is to commiserate over what they didn't receive. Graciousness is the key to enjoying the process of gift registering. Some couples feel uncomfortable registering for gifts, but remember, this is not you asking for presents—it's you making it easier for people who want to buy you a gift to find items that they know you will enjoy.

HOW TO REGISTER • It's important to register as early in the planning process as possible. People begin shopping for wedding gifts long before the wedding, and they also make purchases off the couple's registry list for wedding showers.

Because your gift registry is a service to your guests who may want to buy you presents, consider their needs when deciding where to register. Registering at an obscure store with no method for online ordering, no digital registry, and only one brick-and-mortar location in your town could prove to be not very helpful to your guests. Registering for national and international brands, such as through department stores and home goods stores, is ideal because there is usually a store located nearby for guests who want to shop in person for you and others can comfortably shop online. Registry websites, such as zola.com and newlywish.com, are extra convenient because they allow you to register for a wide range of items from a variety of brands and stores via one online portal for your guests, allow multiple givers to put money toward one gift, offer controlled delivery dates (e.g., not when you're on your honeymoon), and offer a multitude of unique gifts that can't really be wrapped, such as museum memberships, cooking classes, helicopter rides, and wine subscriptions. You are welcome to register anywhere you like, but keep your older, less Internet-savvy guests in mind by setting up at least one registry with a more traditional outlet.

To begin registering for wedding gifts, consider what you would like, what you need, what might be missing from each room of your home, and what would enrich your lives. Whether it's serving ware for dress-up dinner parties, tools for home improvement, or an upgrade on towels and table linens, start there.

LGBTQ+ couples tend to register as a couple and sometimes find themselves disagreeing on styles. Work together with your partner to choose items you will both enjoy, while also registering for selected items that match your individual style. Whether you register as a couple or one of you takes the lead in working on the registry, make sure that you choose gifts that will be used to make your house a home. Personal gift items such as a TV, a new golf bag, or an iPad don't belong on a wedding registry.

The rule of thumb for gift registries is to register for three times the amount of your wedding guest count, to register for items in a variety of price ranges, and to register at two to three national stores. This gives your guests the chance to conveniently shop for gifts at a price point that suits them.

Stay up to date with your registries. If they begin to fill up (or be checked off) faster than you anticipated, you might want to register for more items. This especially tends to happen for couples having multiple wedding showers.

REGISTRY ETIQUETTE 101 • Weddings don't have to be overly stuffy or fussy, but you'll want to balance lightly as you walk the fine tightrope of wedding gift etiquette. Showing good manners about your gifts allows your guests to feel good about celebrating your wedding and also reminds them that you value their presence over presents. But show an ounce of greediness or expectations for gifts and the fun is spoiled for everyone. Remain gracious and keep the following advice in mind.

Word of mouth, your wedding website, your wedding app, and the shower invitation(s) are the best way to tell people about your gift registry. It is verboten to tell your wedding guests where you're registered via your wedding invitation. Share the information verbally only when asked—make sure you're never the one bringing it up.

Guests will seek out where you're registered by asking you, doing their own online search, or asking your family or attendants. Don't worry about making sure they have this information until guests have had enough time to make their own effort to learn where you're registered.

Even a separate enclosure in your wedding invitation envelopes telling guests where you're registered could easily offend them because it places the focus on gifts rather than your desire for their presence at your wedding. (Conversely, telling your guests in the invitation that you don't want any gifts can be equally offensive because it still puts the emphasis on presents, not their presence.)

If you would rather receive money than tangible gifts or experiences, don't mention it unless asked—not even on your wedding website. It's important to note that not everyone likes giving money. So if you're hoping to avoid registries in the hope that people will only give you cash, count that idea out. You might still end up with nonreturnable wares with no gift receipt. Translation: still register for items you'd love for your home so that your guests who want to buy an item to give to you will be more comfortable with their choices.

If a guest does ask about giving you money, say that you and your beloved are saving for a (house, new bedroom set, etc.) and plan to apply any gifts of money you may receive toward that purchase. Be sure to add a courteous comment that any kind of gift your guests decide on will be wonderful.

ALTERNATIVE REGISTRIES

Honeymoon Registries • Honeymoon registries are rising in popularity. The idea here is to create experiences such as massages, day trips, and meals and give guests an opportunity to contribute to them up to certain dollar amounts. You can also include contributions to airfare and lodging. Some guests love this idea, but consider offering a small traditional registry for those guests who do not.

But even some older people are getting hip to what modern couples like, and some of your guests might surprise you with their digital savvy by, say, prepaying for your snorkeling excursion. You can add

There's no minimum or maximum that should be spent on a wedding gift. Ignore the pervasive myth that guests should spend the equivalent of what their dinner costs at the wedding. Not only is that untrue, but your guests should have no idea what your per-head cost is for the wedding. People will buy what they're comfortable purchasing for you, and that is their prerogative.

the link to your honeymoon registry to your wedding website. Be sure to select a website that tracks who gave what for your honeymoon and keep in mind that not all money given will come to you. These sites retain a small percentage for the convenience they deliver.

Charity Registries • Registering for charity donations is popular among LGBTQ+ couples who would rather see money for wedding gifts put back into the community. On your wedding website you can add links to the charities you'd like your guests contributing to in lieu of giving you a wedding gift. Remember, though, that your guests may see this as an option, not a direct request. They might not give to the charity of your choosing, and they still might give you a traditional gift. When they do, accept their gifts graciously, as the gift selection is always up to the wedding guest, not you.

Saying Thank You • It's important to take the time to show gratitude to everyone involved in your wedding, including those who give you gifts, either before or after you say "I do." Handwritten thank-you notes must be sent to each and every person or household who gave you a present. Digital thank-you services, mass video messages, texts, emails, phone calls, and in-person hugs are no substitute for the handwritten note, no matter what technology era we're in. Your loved ones took the time to shop for a meaningful present for you—now take the time to write a meaningful message to them.

Here are some tips for thank-you notes:

- Keep track of all gifts in your worksheets during the entire wedding planning period.
- Use notecards that have your new last name(s) or both your names on the front—not a preprinted thank-you message.
- When you receive shower or engagement gifts, immediately send thank-you notes. Don't wait until after the wedding.
- It's perfectly fine for gift givers to receive more than one thank-you note in the process of your wedding—in fact, ideally, every time they give you a present, you will send them a thank-you note.
- Don't have wedding shower guests fill in their names and addresses on envelopes. That's a lazy way of getting out of the work you need to do yourself.
- You're not too busy to say thank you. Period.
- Send thank-you notes out no more than sixty days after your wedding, but even if you miss the deadline, don't give up—keep on sending them.
- In your card, you should either thank the gift-giver for coming to your wedding or let them know that you missed them at your nuptials. Then mention your excitement over receiving their specific present.
- If they gave you cash, a check, or a gift card, thank the giver for their generous present and mention how you plan to use the money.
- Do not mention that you received a duplicate of their gift or that you might return it.
- Both of you need to sign the thank-you card.
- While not required, consider sending a personal handwritten note of gratitude to any of your vendors who went above and beyond for you on your wedding day.

GIFTS FROM YOU

Going from "I will" to "I do" generally involves a lot of hard work from other people, from family and friends to vendors and venue staff. Giving back to them with presents shows your genuine appreciation for all that they've given to you.

PARENTS • If your parents or other family members have been involved in the wedding planning process, whether by helping you financially or with one or more wedding duties, it's customary to present them with a special gift, such as the following:

- A cooking class
- A gift certificate to their favorite restaurant
- A souvenir from the honeymoon
- Framed photo from your wedding
- Photo album for wedding photos

PARTY HOSTS • Anyone who hosts a wedding shower for you, a rehearsal dinner, an engagement party, a morning-after wedding brunch, or any other gathering should receive a gift from you. Here are some ideas for party host gifts:

- A bouquet of flowers in a vase
- An experience gift, such as a day pass to their favorite museum
- Topiary or plant

ATTENDANTS • Your wedding attendants have given you their time, love, and attention, and often they've spent money on you and your events as well. To show your appreciation, give them each a gift. Your attendants include the flower child and ring bearer. Since your attendants probably range in age and interest, consider giving personalized gifts to each one rather than the same thing to each attendant. Because their duties throughout the wedding are heavier, honor attendants typically receive nicer, more expensive presents.

These gifts are most often given sometime during the wedding weekend—at the rehearsal dinner perhaps, or an event with only your attendants. Here are some ideas on appropriate gift ideas for your attendants:

- A gift certificate to a spa
- A gift certificate to a sporting event or experience
- A monogrammed tote bag
- Cuff links
- Jewelry (Sometimes the jewelry you'd like them to wear on your wedding day, such as a necklace or earrings, can be considered a gift.)

EACH OTHER • Some couples choose to give their mate a gift on their wedding day beyond the exchange of wedding rings. The idea is to memorialize the first day of their marriage with a personalized gift that can be cherished forever, such as:

- A handwritten love letter
- A monogrammed handkerchief
- A watch
- Customized cuff links
- Jewelry engraved with the wedding date

WEDDING FAVORS

Giving small presents to your wedding guests is customary in most corners of the world. The presents needn't be expensive—even a less-expensive wedding favor becomes costly once you multiply it by your guest count. Think of these trinkets as reminders to your guests of how much you appreciate them coming to your wedding.

As you consider possible wedding favors, remember that anything with your wedding date and names permanently on it might end up in a junk drawer until it's whisked away to the donation center or the dump. Modern wedding practice is leaning away from decorative trinkets and more toward favors that are consumable or usable. Keep in mind that many guests will leave their favor behind, because they either forgot it or didn't know it was theirs to take. Whatever you can do to remedy this will be helpful, whether it's having a staff member hand out favors as guests leave or attaching a small note to the favor that thanks the guest for coming and/or has the guest's name written on it.

Here are some ideas for wedding favors:

- A CD with a selection of your wedding reception music
- A personalized item that doubles as a place-card holder, such as a bejeweled picture frame
- A take-home bag of candy at your dessert station (Be sure to have a sign that tells your guests to take candy home with them.)
- Individual bottles of liquor or wine
- Labeled jelly jars of your own preserves or pickled vegetables
- Packets of seeds
- Printed photos from the photo booth
- Small potted plants

Tasks to Tackle

- ☐ Register for wedding gifts. (Don't be surprised if this takes more than one day.)
- ☐ Create a spreadsheet to keep track of received presents.
- ☐ Make a list of everyone you'll be giving a gift to.
- ☐ A month before the wedding, check your registry to see if you need to add more items.
- ☐ Shop for gifts early to be sure you have time to pick out something thoughtful.
- ☐ Don't use any wedding presents until after you've gotten married. If the wedding is canceled, all gifts need to be returned.

CHAPTER TWENTY

ATTIRE

Selecting your wedding attire is one of the most fulfilling parts of planning your celebration. Styling your wedding showcases your personalities as a couple and represents how you view yourselves, and the same goes for the clothing and accessories you don on the day. Because you are dressing for yourself—and your mate—your wedding outfit should be comfortable, but it should also be an outward expression of your personality and gender expression, while mirroring the overall look and feel of your wedding. So, no pressure!

For instance, an intricately beaded gown with a long train might not be appropriate for a backyard wedding at 3:00 p.m. And if your reception is going to be held in a luxury ballroom at a five-star resort, you wouldn't show up in a pair of linen pants and flip-flops. Everything—attire included—should fit in with your wedding style, from venue to season to location. You're going for flow and a seamless presentation. This chapter will give you some guidelines to finding the ensemble of your dreams.

LOVE WHAT YOU WEAR

Shopping for attire is thrilling to some while daunting to others, especially those who dress one way in their everyday lives but feel pressured to dress another way for their wedding day. If you're feeling that pressure, let me remind you: Your wedding day is the time for you to shine and enjoy yourself. Wear clothes that make you feel proud to stand up in front of your beloved and vow to love, honor, and cherish them for the rest of your days. If you're uncomfortable in your outfit, it's going to show on your face and in your body. On your wedding day, you should be filled to the brim with radiating happiness. Let it beam all around you by loving your attire.

OFF-THE-RACK, MADE-TO-ORDER, OR TAILORED?

Styles differ between dress designers and suit makers—some are geared toward slender figures, while others cater to more substantial people. Off-the-rack suits and dresses work perfectly fine for cisgender individuals whose gender identity matches their body. But it might not suit a nonbinary person or a trans man who is wearing a chest binder and does not want to showcase their hourglass waist or curvy hips. For more on this, see clothier Mary Going's essay on page 214. Made-to-order and fully customized suits and gowns are more expensive, but having wedding attire that fits you well is priceless.

PAIRING FABRICS

Whether or not the two of you are wearing a similar style of clothing, your photos will work best if your fabrics are complementary in weight and color. If one of you is wearing a heavy, embroidered, ivory princess gown and the other is wearing a lightweight, bright-diamond-white silk sheath, not only might your photos look off (the ivory gown may very well end up looking yellowed, old, or even dingy), but whenever you come together for a kiss or a dance the embroidery on the gown is likely to snag the silk fabric of the sheath.

KNOW THY BUDGET

You should already know the range of costs you're planning on for your entire outfit, including a price range specifically for a gown if either of you is buying one. When you're calling for appointments, don't be shy about asking about their price range for gowns. It's been many a budget-conscious nearlywed's downfall to try on a dress that they couldn't afford.

SHOP EARLY

Don't leave wedding attire shopping until the end—even if you're trying to get into better shape for your wedding. Not only does it take anywhere from six weeks to six months for truly custom dresses and suits to be completed, but you'll also need time for fittings and adjustments. And that's after you find the perfect marrying outfit. Between all the other appointments you'll be juggling while planning your wedding and trying to carry on with your regular life, make time to go try on a variety of dresses or suits to find the right fit.

FASHION-FORWARD

I encourage you to mix it up. On equallywed.com, we feature real weddings of celebrants wearing masculine suits topped with a veil or a floor-length cape. Conversely, we regularly feature brides, brooms, and grooms in three-piece suits carrying a bouquet instead of wearing a boutonniere. The day is yours—the more you love your style, the better able you'll be to rock the aisle like a runway.

GOWNS, JUMPSUITS, PANTSUITS, AND DRESSES

To determine the style of dress you want, let's first discuss your options. A wedding gown is a formal type of dress, usually floor-length. If it's shorter, it might be called simply a dress (as opposed to a gown), but truly this is just a matter of semantics. Wedding gowns come in a variety of silhouettes, necklines, and fabrics. Listed here are the ones you're most likely to find in your gown shopping.

GOWN SILHOUETTES

- **A-line**: A fitted bodice gradually spreading out into the shape of an A forms this classic bridal look.
- **Ball gown or princess**: This is a regal dress silhouette boasting a slim-cut bodice that trims the waist and then blooms out into a full bell shape.
- **Empire**: The bodice in empire-waist gowns is fitted down to just below the bust, and then the fabric flows out from there.

- **Jumpsuit**: This top-and-pants combo is sewn together but is anything but casual when created with the right fabrics and cut. The pant style varies from palazzo to skinny to cropped.
- **Mermaid or trumpet**: The elongated bodice of a mermaid hugs your body all the way down to below your hips and then flares out either midthigh (trumpet) or just below the knees (mermaid).
- **Pantsuit**: Separate matching jacket and pants.
- **Peplum**: The silhouette of a wedding gown becomes a peplum style when a short overskirt or ruffle is sewn onto the waistline.
- **Sheath**: This sleek design offers long, straight lines, making for a modern look for slim figures.
- **Short**: Cropped hemlines can be above the knee, knee-length, or tea-length (midcalf).

GOWN NECKLINES

- **Bateau**: This wide, straight-across neckline is higher up on the chest and covers more of the inner shoulders.
- **Cowl**: The fabric gathers across the chest in soft piles.
- **Halter**: The dress straps are linked in the back.
- **High neck**: The fabric completely covers the breast and a small portion of the neck.
- **Illusion**: Transparent fabric is used above the bust to create the illusion that the neckline is higher.
- **Jewel**: A rounded neckline at the collarbones.
- **Off-shoulder**: The fabric is used to create the appearance of the straps being casually draped around the tops of the arms instead of on the shoulders.
- **One-shoulder**: This asymmetric look is achieved with the dress cut to have only one shoulder strap.
- **Scoop**: A U-shaped neckline.
- **Square**: A square-shaped neckline with rounded corners. A neckline with unrounded corners—that is, with the angles as connected straight lines—is called "court."

- **Strapless**: A dress or top with no shoulder straps and typically a straight cut across the bust unless otherwise specified.
- **Sweetheart**: The fabric over the bust resembles the top two curves of a heart. A sweetheart neckline is usually strapless, but sometimes the effect is paired with spaghetti straps, halter straps, or an illusion neckline.
- **V-neck**: Plunging or not, the fabric forms a V in the middle of the breasts.

VEILS • You'll want your veil and attire fabrics to be compatible. If your gown or suit is more structured, go for a stiffer veil. Similarly, a softer outfit made with draping fabric might look best with a thinner, gauzier veil. Listed here are the popular veil lengths:

- **Birdcage**: This retro veil is short and covers only the face.
- **Blusher**: A veil—or a portion thereof—that is worn until you're in front of your mate at the front of the ceremony space, when it's traditionally moved back.
- **Elbow**: A veil that reaches to your elbow.
- **Fingertip**: This midbody-length veil reaches your fingertips.
- **Cathedral**: The longest and most formal veil, the cathedral is usually the length of your gown's train.
- **Chapel**: This veil reaches the bottom of your gown.

GOWN FABRICS AND FINISHES
- **Alençon lace**: This distinct floral pattern boasts an instantly recognizable corded detail.
- **Batiste**: This lightweight, soft, yet strong transparent fabric is woven with cotton or linen.
- **Brocade**: This Jacquard-woven fabric has raised designs.
- **Chantilly lace**: This lace is built on a netting base and then topped with flowers and ribbon made out of thread.
- **Charmeuse**: Light, semi-lustrous, delicate, and soft, this form-fitting textile feels like satin.

- **Chiffon:** This transparent fabric is sheer without the sheen.
- **Crepe:** A light, soft, and thin fabric with a crinkled surface.
- **Damask:** Similar to brocade with its raised designs, damask is woven in a much lighter weight.
- **Duchesse satin:** A lightweight cross between silk and rayon or polyester woven into a satin finish.
- **Dupioni:** This popular, slightly iridescent silk blend is sometimes referred to as shantung. Dupioni boasts raised fibers, however, making it thicker and rougher than shantung.
- **Faille:** A structured silk with a glossy, finely ribbed, woven look, faille can also be made from cotton or synthetic fabrics.
- **Gabardine:** A tightly woven fabric with a firm and durable finish.
- **Georgette:** Crepelike and super-lightweight, this sheer matte fabric is often made of polyester or silk.
- **Jersey:** An elastic knit fabric.
- **Moire:** A heavy, crisp silk taffeta with a waterlike appearance, moire is a common fabric used in vintage gowns.
- **Organdy/organza:** Organdy is made of cotton and organza is made of silk, but both fabrics are extremely sheer and crisp. The crisp texture creates volume, so they're often used to fill full-skirted gowns.
- **Peau de soie:** A soft satin with a dull luster and a grainy appearance.
- **Pique:** A knit fabric with a waffle-weave appearance.
- **Polyester:** An inexpensive synthetic fiber that can be woven into just about anything, including lace and satin.
- **Rayon:** An elastic and more affordable version of silk.
- **Satin:** A supportive, smooth, and heavy fabric.
- **Shantung:** Shantung's rubbed texture resembles raw silk. It's slightly smoother than dupioni.
- **Silk:** The cherished natural fiber of true silk makes it expensive. Silk comes in multiple varieties, including gazar and mikado.
- **Silk gazar (or gazaar):** Silk gazar is a heavy, sheer, four-ply silk organza fabric with a smooth texture and crisp, matte finish.

- **Silk mikado:** Mikado is a type of silk weaving that creates luster; it's sometimes made from less-expensive synthetic fabrics.
- **Silk-faced satin:** A smooth silk satin that's glossy on the front and matte on the back.
- **Taffeta:** Crisp and smooth, this fabric can be made from silk or rayon.
- **Tulle:** Ballerina-like netting made of silk, nylon, or rayon.
- **Velvet:** A soft, thick fabric, velvet is plush on the front and plain on the underside.

DRESS SHOPPING • The excitement of donning a wedding gown never gets old, but your heart might flutter even more the first time you try one on. This is one of the most important dresses you'll ever wear (no pressure, right?), and you'll want to feel and look as amazing as possible. Whether you're buying off the rack or going couture—or somewhere in between—begin by browsing wedding dresses early. Gather the styles you're drawn to either on a digital board of images or in a binder with tear sheets from magazines. See how real people wear them in wedding editorials. Look for images of marriers with your body shape to see how their gowns fit them.

Once you're ready to start trying on wedding gowns, follow these ten tips:

1. Find LGBTQ-friendly wedding salons on equallywed.com or through word of mouth. Nothing dampens the day like hearing homophobic or transphobic remarks from the staff.

2. Make your appointments for times when the stores are less busy, either early in the morning or on weekdays, so that you'll have both more space to move about and quiet time for musing over each gown. If you try on gowns when the store is busy, you run the risk of hearing random shoppers lovingly oohing and aahing over you. That can feel good, but it's also confusing when you're trying to make a decision.

3. Bring a maximum of three people with you to give you feedback. With a bigger group you'll have too many differing opinions, which can be discouraging rather than encouraging.

4. Although it's completely okay to bring along your spouse-to-be, and the choice is completely up to you, know that it can be wonderful to have your outfit be a surprise for the day of your wedding.

5. If you're both wearing gowns or female-bodied suits, you don't necessarily have to shop together, but do discuss the shades and fabrics of your attire so that you'll complement each other. Either bring along the same friend or family member so that someone will know what both gowns look like or have the same style consultant at the same shop assist both of you on separate days.

6. Most bridal salons do not keep every color and size in stock, so be prepared to try on a sample, which will be clipped in the back.

7. You can save money by buying a sample dress, but you might end up spending a fortune in cleaning and alterations.

8. Custom wedding gowns take anywhere from five to eight months to come in, whereas off-the-rack dresses are available either the same day or within four weeks.

9. Wedding gown sizes typically run one or two sizes smaller than other clothes, so focus on your measurements, not the size number.

10. You don't have to buy a "wedding" dress. Cocktail dresses and other formalwear can make for a gorgeous look on your wedding day.

· · ·

Q: I'm a trans woman getting married, and I'm concerned about the dress-shopping experience. I haven't yet had my breasts built, but I don't want to be shamed at bridal boutiques. How can I manage all of this and yet still be treated like the queen I know I am?

a: Congratulations on your upcoming marriage, your highness! First of all, the right shop will be sensitive to your specific needs. To find such a shop, search for equality-minded wedding vendors on equallywed.com. We list companies that not only have vowed to treat every person with equal respect, no matter their gender presentation or sexual orientation, but also have received education on being sensitive to the specific needs of LGBTQ+ people.

To take the focus off of your body and the transition, prepare yourself at home before going to the dress shop. If this means donning a bra with breast inserts or pads before you go out, do so. Many trans women have a larger chest circumference, which results in a larger band size that's not always compatible with the cup sizes of the dresses in stock. For this reason, it might be best to start shopping for custom gowns or at stores that stock larger sample sizes. If you're on hormones for growth, advise your dress consultant and/or your seamstress or seamster that your cup size might grow more before your wedding day. They might be able to build in a bit of safety fabric to let out closer to your wedding. If you're uncomfortable discussing this with a stranger, bring a friend to soothe your nerves and research each store on your behalf before you visit.

SHOES • Modern marriers are stepping out in an assortment of fun footwear. Some still prefer the classic white or ivory high heel, but pairing your gown, dress, pantsuit, or jumpsuit with sandals, flats, wedges, cowboy boots, Toms, Converses, or Doc Martens can add comfort while being playful and still fashionable. You can even swap out your shoes for the reception. Try to wear the shoes you'll be getting married in to your fittings to ensure the correct length for your dress or pants. And practice walking around your home in your new shoes—especially ones with height—not only to break them in but to make sure you don't topple over during the ceremony.

SUITS

Shopping for your picture-perfect wedding suit is your chance to trot out your most debonair sense of style, to look as dashing and tremendously handsome as you feel. Whether one or both of you are wearing suits on your wedding day, consider each other's choices in hues and fabrics when shopping for your own attire. If you don't want to reveal your outfit to your sweetheart before the big day, have the same person shop with each of you, or use the same suit maker, to ensure that your outfits coordinate well for photos and overall aesthetics.

You'll have other elements to ponder while putting together your wedding ensemble, such as how formal you want your attire to be, the color, the cut, and the accessories.

FORMAL ATTIRE • Plan on dressing as formal as you are asking your guests to be, if not a notch higher. If your guests are likely to don sundresses and linen pants and Cuban shirts for your beach wedding, kick it up a level by wearing a linen suit. If you're tying the knot in the ballroom of an upscale wedding venue and you've put "black tie" on the invitations, wear something more formal.

TUXEDOS VS. SUITS • Suiting up in a tuxedo makes almost anyone instantly sophisticated. However, the classic suit can be equally elegant, formal, and exquisite, as long as it's been altered to fit your body. Both suits and tuxes can be rented or purchased, but the less standard your body type and style is, the more important it is to have it made to your exact measurements. Even if you rent your suit or tux online, have your measurements taken professionally or have your spouse-to-be watch a useful how-to video before attempting this for the first time.

Cummerbunds are worn without a belt underneath, with pleats facing up, and in place of a vest or waistcoat. Match it to your tie.

SUIT JACKETS • The style of a formal jacket truly makes the suit's personality come to life. Vents—the opening at the back of the jacket—are a critical consideration when selecting a wedding jacket. Ventless jackets offer a slimmer look, but double side vents give you more room to move on the dance floor. Single-breasted and double-breasted tuxedo jackets boast satin accents. The double-breasted jacket is always worn closed, without a vest or a cummerbund.

Despite the common opinion that the tuxedo is the most formal option, tuxedos are actually a semiformal dinner jacket paired with matching trousers. If you want to go all out formal, wear a tailcoat—a jacket with tails. Stroller jackets are cut gradually longer from the wrist to the back, where they hit the back of the knees. Morning coats are a handsome formal option for a daytime wedding. These have a closer fit than a sports coat and a more tailored look than a blazer.

The key to making your outfit a suit instead of merely a jacket and pants is to have the jacket match the pants exactly in hue and fabric. Jackets with tails are typically worn at incredibly formal evening weddings (though we've featured on equallywed.com a groom wearing a white tuxedo jacket with tails under a white-and-purple satin cathedral veil at a daytime church wedding). A sleek formal look is the three-piece suit ensemble, which elevates the elegance of a basic suit by matching it with a vest.

SUIT FABRICS • Suits are made in a variety of fabrics. In determining which one of the following common suit fabrics works best for you, consider the season and location of your wedding:

- **Cashmere:** Although it gives suit jackets a luxurious feeling, cashmere is not as durable as other fabrics.
- **Linen:** An extremely lightweight option, linen is meant for spring and summer use. One downside with linen is that it's prone to wrinkling.
- **Seersucker:** A thin form of cotton, seersucker is lightweight with a distinct ribbed texture.
- **Silk:** True silk is a luxury, and it makes for a soft and breathable jacket.
- **Tweed:** A medium to heavyweight fabric, tweed is a rough-surfaced woolen wool, typically of mixed flecked colors.
- **Worsted wool:** Made from yarn, this heavyweight option is thinner and rougher than woolen wool.

SHOES • The footwear you select will depend largely on your attire, but the season, the region, and the formality of your wedding should be considered as well. For a formal look, suits look best with slick patent-leather lace-ups, oxfords, or brogues, but Converses, stylish sneakers, cowboy boots, or other playful shoes can bring an unexpected and fun air to your wedding. Dress boots can be worn in cold or inclement weather, and dress loafers or monk straps are acceptable if you're dressing the suit down by forgoing a tie. If you're marrying on the beach, your best bets are sandals, boat shoes, or canvas shoes—or going barefoot.

Make sure you break in your shoes by wearing them around your house to avoid cuts, blisters, and slipping on your wedding day. And bring them to your fittings to ensure accurate measurements of your trousers.

IN A BIND

If you bind your chest to reduce the appearance of breasts, make sure to:

1. **Purchase a real binder.** Medical or sports bandages can become tighter the longer they're worn, restricting your ability to breathe, or, depending on the fabric, they can loosen, increasing the chance of a strange bulkiness appearing under your shirt while you're cutting a rug on the dance floor.

How to Tie a Bow Tie

1. Start with the bow tie lying face up. Adjust the bow tie so that the right side is shorter than the left. The end on the left will be referred to as A and the end on the right will be referred to as B.

2. Move A to the right side, across B.

3. Bring A under B and up through the neck loop.

4. At the joint, fold B toward the right and then toward the left to create the bow shape.

5. Bring A straight down over the middle of the bow shape that was made with B.

6. Fold A back toward the chest and pinch the fold.

7. Push the pinched end (A) through the loop behind B.

8. Pull on the folded parts of the bow to tighten.

9. Adjust until balanced on both sides.

2. **Stick with a reputable binder manufacturer.** Only a good binder will give you the best and safest fit.

3. **Avoid buying a smaller binder.** Wearing a binder that's too small won't just make your chest flatter—it could also severely damage your ribs and lungs, creating medical issues when your true focus is on getting married.

4. **Stay cool.** Remember that binders can get hot, so shop for a shirt that's even more breathable to make up for the heat you're adding to your outfit. If your wedding will be held in a warm climate, you should also consider marrying in an (air-conditioned) indoor space. You can also bring a second dress shirt for the reception (especially if you're a heavy sweater in general).

Suiting Up

GUEST EXPERT: MARY GOING

clothing designer and entrepreneur, Oakland, California

Your memories of your wedding day will last a lifetime, not only in your mind but in photos and videos too. It's important that you look and feel your best, not only for the big day but also when you enjoy these timeless artifacts and memorabilia.

If your dream is to wear a suit, know that the vast majority of ready-to-wear suiting is made for bodies with broad shoulders, long torsos, narrow hips, and no breasts. If that description doesn't fit you, you may need a custom suit.

Plan in advance! A custom suit is just that: custom-made for you. It takes time. The process typically starts with a fitting. At that first visit, you'll get measured and pick fabric, lining, and other details of the suit. Once the suit is made, you'll have a final fitting, which will include accommodation for any weight loss or gain, the hemming of the pants, and any other slight alterations that need to be made.

It's very unlikely that you could be properly fitted from a distance. If you happen to live in a city with a suiting company that is meant to serve you, it's best to use them. You're almost guaranteed to have a better experience because of their assumptions about you and about your body. If such a company isn't available, and if traveling is not possible, you'll need to get a little more creative.

First, understand the different ways a suit can be made. Made-for-you suits are generically called "custom," but in fact most are not entirely custom-made. Most clothing is made with basic assumptions about the wearer's body that may or may not fit your particular shape. If you've ever bought a men's shirt and could not button the bottom button, you understand how wrong these assumptions can be!

A truly custom tailor will make no assumptions and will make a suit for your body, based entirely on your body's shape and size. These master tailors are in very short supply, and a suit made by a master tailor should cost thousands of dollars. If it costs less than that, it's not custom-made, but rather "made to measure."

A made-to-measure suit is still made just for you, and it's the right solution for most people, but you have to be careful about those assumptions. The fewer measurements the person makes, the more assumptions they are making, and unless you're shopping in a women-specific environment, chances are that those assumptions will be based on cis male proportions. This is the main reason that shopping online, or from a distance, is not likely to produce good results.

Sometimes distance or online shopping can produce good results. But the more difficulty you have with regular clothes shopping, the more likely it is that you should visit a professional tailor in person.

Well-made suits are easily tailored after the fact, so you can buy with confidence that you'll be able to wear the pieces for many years, even if you are prone to weight fluctuations.

The fabric and all the details are completely up to you and should be dictated solely by your desire to feel confident when you walk down the aisle. Having said that, if this is your first suit, and if you plan to wear it on other occasions after your wedding, I suggest buying a neutral color—either charcoal or navy. Many people are tempted by black. Black is best suited for weddings and funerals, but it's too severe for most other occasions. A charcoal or navy suit will be absolutely perfect. If it seems boring, think of all the wonderful shirts and ties you can spruce it up with—those will cost a great deal less than a whole new suit.

While you're buying your suit, you should also get a custom shirt made. Men's dress shirts are made to fit a cis male body and are likely to be either too big in the neck or too small in the chest. And if you're not a cis male, the sleeves will almost inevitably be too long. Plus there's that bottom button issue.

Buying a suit doesn't have to be traumatic. Plan early: your first visit with the tailor should be four to six months in advance. Look at Pinterest. Read online reviews. You know how to do this! The most important thing is to feel great on your amazing day.

ATTENDANT ATTIRE

Finding the perfect wedding dress or suit for yourself can be stressful enough, so adding the pursuit of the perfect dresses or suits for your attendants can feel overwhelming. Navigating a myriad of personalities and different style preferences, nearlyweds often find the process more difficult than they anticipated. However, many of the challenging elements can be dealt with swiftly and smoothly with a little foresight.

START EARLY • Coordinating attendants and their attire purchases can be tough on any couple, but if you begin the process at least seven to eight months before the wedding, you'll worry less about having time to finish alterations. Giving yourself a time cushion also allows you to shop around for better prices or watch for sales.

MONEY TALKS • One sensitive subject for almost everyone is personal finances. It's important to understand how much each member of your wedding party can afford to spend on attire in order to avoid disruptions in your planning process. Don't make assumptions—be up front with each one privately to find out what they might be able to budget. Armed with this information, you'll be better able to determine your browsing price point.

DO YOUR OWN RESEARCH • Get an idea of the aesthetic you want your attendants' outfits to reflect before pulling them into the process. Style, fabric, color, size, and cut options abound, so narrow the decision down to a few choices before presenting them to the party.

GIVE YOUR ATTENDANTS DIRECTION • If you're considering letting attendants wear something of their own choosing, direct them toward the color, fabric, silhouette, and level of formality that you desire. This is as much about you getting what you want as it is about helping them look their best.

SHOP TOGETHER • Retailers often provide a discount if you can purchase all the dresses or suits in one place around the same time. Shopping together also ensures quality control.

Tasks to Tackle

- Shop for your attire six to eight months before the big day.
- Plan for two to four fittings.
- Wear your wedding shoes to your fittings.
- Coordinate your fabric and shade with your partner's.
- Write down all your appointments for fittings and final pickup.
- Make a note of when your attendants need to pick up their attire (in case they need a gentle reminder).

CHAPTER TWENTY-ONE

RINGS

Many couples enjoy following tradition by exchanging rings. Wedding rings are sometimes presented at the engagement, but they can also be selected during the wedding planning period. The circles of your wedding rings indicate eternity, and that's how long you should plan on wearing them. The gravity of this purchase calls for sensible planning. And you're going to want to fall head over heels in love with your rings.

HOW TO SHOP FOR WEDDING RINGS

SHOP EARLY • Whether you're browsing in person or online, give yourself ample time to think about designs, and don't forget to build a cushion into the timeline for ring sizing, engraving, and the insurance purchase. Begin looking for your wedding bands at least two months before your wedding date. Allow even more time if you're interested in a custom ring. Keep in mind that engraving can take up to one month.

ORDER THE RIGHT SIZE • Trying on rings after a particularly salty meal or post-workout might lead you to purchase a bigger ring than you need on a regular basis. Try on wedding rings at a time of day when your fingers are at their most average size.

SET A BUDGET • Simple gold bands can cost as low as $125. At the low end, platinum bands start between $400 and $600. Wedding bands with diamonds can set you back from upwards of $800 to staggeringly high digits, depending on the metal and the quality of the diamonds, as well as the designer. And then there's engraving, which ranges in cost from $1 to $15 per character (letter or number), depending on the font and whether the engraving is done by hand or machine.

USE AN EQUALITY-MINDED JEWELER • Nothing dampens the spirits quite like a jeweler asking if one of you is the best man or the maid of honor. To lessen this possibility, only shop for rings from jewelers who are known to support the LGBTQ+ community. For more on locating equality-minded wedding vendors, refer to page 66 or visit equallywed.com.

USE ONLY CONFLICT-FREE DIAMONDS • If you're adding diamonds to your engagement or wedding rings, make sure the stones are "conflict-free." "Conflict" diamonds are illicitly mined stones that fund criminal activity in the world's war zones. You can find conflict-free diamonds by working with jewelers who adhere to the Kimberley Process, a joint effort among governments, industry, and society to halt the flow of conflict diamonds.

However, the KP can't help anyone avoid the large number of diamonds tainted by violence, human rights abuses, poverty, and environmental degradation. If you don't want your bling surrounded by ecological or ethical questions, consider a synthetic stone or a recycled diamond from a family heirloom or vintage piece, or work only with a diamond dealer who can guarantee ethically sourced stones.

THINK ABOUT MATERIALS • It's entirely up to you whether you have matching rings, rings that simply complement each other, or rings that look nothing alike. Your choice will largely be determined by the materials used in making your rings. Wedding bands are designed in a variety of materials, which include but aren't limited to:

- **Cobalt:** Made from a highly durable alloy, cobalt is a bright white metal that is much harder than platinum yet less dense.
- **Gold:** Pure 100 percent gold is 24 karat by definition, but it's too soft for everyday wear.
- **Palladium:** A naturally white metal, palladium is hypoallergenic, will not tarnish, and remains white forever. This is one of the more rare metals available.
- **Platinum:** This durable yet rare metal maintains a white sheen.
- **Rose gold:** A combination of gold, copper, and silver.
- **Sterling silver:** Pure silver, also called fine silver, is relatively soft, supple, and easily damaged, so it's commonly combined with other metals to produce a more durable product. The most popular of these alloys is sterling silver, which consists of 92.5 percent silver and 7.5 percent copper.
- **Titanium:** A pale shade of gray, titanium rings feel lighter than either gold or platinum and are incredibly durable because they're typically made from almost pure titanium. Titanium is such a strong material, however, that it's difficult for jewelers to resize titanium rings.
- **Tungsten:** A strong material, tungsten carbide is a forged metal created from an alloy of elemental tungsten and carbon alloyed with other metals.
- **Vermeil:** Though it has a rich golden color, vermeil is actually a sterling silver plated with gold.
- **White gold:** White gold is an alloy of gold and at least one white metal, such as nickel, manganese, or palladium. Like yellow gold, the purity of white gold is given in karats.
- **Wood:** Wooden wedding bands are gaining popularity, though their ability to last a lifetime is questionable.
- **Yellow gold:** Yellow gold is created with natural pure gold and color-saturated alloys, such as copper with a red hue and silver featuring a green hue.

DO A QUALITY CHECK • Confirm that the inside of each wedding band has two marks: the manufacturer's trademark, which signifies that the company stands behind its work, and the quality mark (24K or PLAT, for example), which indicates that the metal is what the jeweler claims it is. If the ring consists of two or more metals, make sure there is a quality mark for each.

Tasks to Tackle

- Browse wedding rings
- Research wedding ring jewelers.
- If you're interested, ask family members whether any heirloom rings are available.
- Try on a variety of rings.
- Purchase rings.
- Insure rings.
- Store rings somewhere safe.

CHAPTER TWENTY-TWO

YOUR WEDDING DAY

Today's the day you've been working so hard for! You're almost married. Try to enjoy every moment leading up to the most exquisite moment of the day: looking into your beloved's eyes, blissfully knowing you've found someone whom you treasure and who treasures you, and vowing your love forever. Here are some tips to help ensure that the day of your wedding goes smoothly.

PLAN AHEAD

No matter how relaxed you are in your daily life, it pays to make wedding day plans for yourself and everyone involved. Have an exact schedule and timeline for where everyone—you, family members, helpers, attendants, and vendors—need to be and what everyone's roles are. (If you have hired a wedding planner or a day-of coordinator, they'll take care of all this.) The schedule should include everything from who will crown your wedding cake with the topper to who is making sure everyone has their bouquets and boutonnieres, to how you'll be getting to the ceremony, to reminding your DJ when to start playing music. Stay organized, be a communicative leader, ask for help, take deep breaths, and count to 10 if you start to feel overwhelmed or

frustrated (sometimes you might need to keep going to 100). Arming anyone with a role to play with a detailed itinerary of what happens when and who executes what helps everything go smoothly.

If you know your beloved is notoriously bad with time management, assign someone else to keep an eye on the schedule for them. And make sure to cushion your time. For example, if you and your attendants are getting your makeup and hair professionally done, don't assume that everyone will be taken care of by separate stylists or makeup artists. Plan on one to one and one-half hours for your hair if you're having an up-do or getting heavily styled and forty-five minutes for each of your attendants to have their hair done. The same goes for makeup applications.

Taking turns with the hair and makeup artists could take several hours to get everyone done, so start earlier in the day and plan accordingly. And remember: allowing time to enjoy the preparation process will not only reduce your stress but give you happy time with your best friends and loved ones.

PACK A BAG

So that all personal emergencies can be easily taken care of, bring all your essentials to the place where you're getting ready. Use this handy list to make sure you've got everything you need with you:

- Attire: every item in your wedding ensemble, including gowns, suits, dress shirt (and a backup for the reception), binders, ties, ceremony shoes, comfortable reception shoes, special shapewear, lingerie, hosiery, veils, headwear, and all accessories
- Baby powder (it soaks up sweat!)
- Band-Aids for blisters or small cuts
- Bobby pins or hair fasteners for any up-dos that fall or to redo your hair if changes in the weather force you to rethink your hairstyle
- Button-up shirt to wear while your hair is styled and makeup is applied (it'll be easier to disrobe afterward without messing anything up)
- Cologne or perfume (apply sparingly)
- Comb or brush
- Contact case and cleaner
- Cosmetics for touch-ups, even if you're having your makeup professionally done
- Deodorant
- Deodorant removal wipes/sponges
- Eye drops for red eyes or allergy attacks
- Glasses, glass cleaner, and glasses case
- Hair gel
- Hair spray
- Handkerchief or pack of tissues

- Itinerary for the day in either digital or printed form, but with hard copies for everyone involved
- Labeled envelopes with check and cash gratuities for vendors as well as final payments for vendors (see page 35 for a guide to who and how much to tip), to be distributed by your wedding planner or a sincerely trusted family member or friend
- Love letter to hand to your spouse on the day of your wedding
- Makeup or baby wipes for last-minute mistakes
- Marriage license, ketubah, or both
- Mints
- Nail file and clippers for any last-minute snags
- Nail polish remover (in a sealed bottle); nail polish that matches the color you're wearing; clear nail polish for any tears in hosiery
- Overnight bag for your wedding night (consider packing lingerie or sexy undies to surprise your new spouse, as well as any other supplies you know you'll enjoy)
- Pain relief: either acetaminophen or ibuprofen
- Phone
- Phone or iPad programmed with a fun playlist for getting ready with your attendants as well as a separate sexy playlist for your wedding night
- Phone charger
- Prescription medication you need to take the day or night of your wedding (or the morning after)
- Printed items that you're responsible for delivering to the venue, such as ceremony programs, place cards, escort cards, menus to be set at place settings, and the guest book
- Q-tips
- Safety pins
- Sewing kit for any fabric emergencies
- Snacks like small bags of almonds, granola bars, or other small bits of protein (they're great for maintaining your energy before your ceremony, and many a couple has devoured these snacks in a

late-night frenzy in their wedding night hotel room after forgetting to eat at their ceremony)

- Stain remover wipes or sticks
- Tampons or pads
- Tweezers
- Wedding rings

TAKE GOOD CARE OF YOURSELF

DON'T FORGET TO EAT • On the morning of your wedding day (or in the afternoon if you're marrying in the evening), plan on eating a full breakfast and lunch packed with protein, no matter how afraid you are of bulging out in your wedding attire. You need energy to sustain yourself. Plus, attendants might be slipping you glasses of bubbly (or shots), either to celebrate with you or to calm your nerves. Drinking on an empty stomach is a surefire way to get drunk or sick before your vows, neither of which you want. Plan on drinking plenty of water throughout the day so that you'll feel your best at your ceremony.

KEEP YOUR BEAUTY AND GROOMING REGIMEN GENTLE
Of course you're going to shower on your wedding day for the ultimate freshness, but today's not the day to try out any type of new acne remedy, face mask, scrub, or treatments, a new razor, or, if you have especially sensitive skin, even new makeup. Use what you know has proven results in order to avoid a blotchy face, razor burn, cuts, or worse.

ALL THE SEEMINGLY SMALL THINGS ON THE DAY OF

FLOWERS • As you'll have arranged with your florist, your flowers should arrive at the area where you're getting ready. Have a helper pass them out to the appropriate people, and handle them with care to maintain their pristine condition for your ceremony.

HOW TO PIN THE BOUTONNIERE • Your wedding might be the first time you've donned a bout. As mentioned earlier, a boutonniere doesn't go through the buttonhole of your lapel, in spite of the original

French meaning of the word. Rather, it should be pinned just above the buttonhole with the stem facing downward. (The florist should provide the pins.) Push the pin through the left lapel from the back. Push the pin through the widest part of the boutonniere. Then push it back through the lapel. Make sure that both the pinhead (even if it's a pearl) and the tip are out of sight.

GETTING READY • An increasing number of LGBTQ+ couples are choosing to get ready together, especially if they don't have attendants, or not that many. Whatever arrangement you choose, make sure you have an assigned space for getting ready and, if desired, plan to have the photographer come toward the end while finishing touches are being made. Some of the most treasured wedding photos come from moments when the couple is getting ready—such as a bow tie or veil going on with the help of a loved one, or shoes being tied—and the happy anticipation can be seen on everyone's faces.

BE PRESENT

Today is your wedding day! Numerous brides, brooms, and grooms look back on their wedding day with warm hearts but fuzzy memories. With so much going on, the hundreds of micro conversations, the details everywhere you look, and the rush of emotions, naturally it'll be a blur to some extent. Even if your reception is scheduled for three to five hours, it will go by faster than you can imagine. Giving the day the significant gift of being present allows you to retain more memories and enjoy yourself even more.

TEN WAYS TO BE A MINDFUL MARRIER

1. Before heading to the ceremony space, spend two to ten minutes alone for a brief meditation.

2. Set an intention to be purposefully mindful at both the ceremony and the reception. Just calling your wish into existence places it at the center of your mind.

3. If someone important to you is not attending, whether by choice or because of distance, illness, or death, send out vibes of love, affection, and forgiveness to them for their absence. It can absolutely hurt to marry without someone you'd always hoped would be there for you on your wedding day, and you deserve the chance to express that grief. Once you release those feelings, it will be easier to carry that person in your heart during your wedding— and easier to focus on the people who *are* there for you.

4. Take time to look into people's eyes and connect with each of your guests.

5. Let the staff do their jobs. Focus on enjoying your celebration instead of managing it.

6. If you're imbibing alcohol, drink a full glass of water in between beers, glasses of wine, or cocktails. The alcohol isn't going anywhere, and the more you drink, the less likely you are to remember everything about your wedding.

7. Steal some sweet time with your new spouse. With everyone rushing up to you to give you their best wishes, it can be easy to get separated at the party. Come back together as often as you can to reconnect.

8. Tell a dear friend or even your planner or photographer that you want to stay present and ask them to remind you of any moments you hoped to have at your reception, such as dancing

with an aging relative, or getting a photo of you with your oldest friend or just closing your eyes and concentrating on hearing the good energy.

9. Every now and then stop talking, take a deep breath, and look around you. Everyone you love has come to celebrate your happiness. Soak it in. Feel the love. Savor the present of being present.

10. Sit down and eat something. Running around at your wedding can feel like you're on a never-ending merry-go-round. That may be an awesome feeling, but then when it's all over, it's done. Sitting down and taking the time to eat will help you get stabilized in the moment.

Tasks to Tackle

- Make sure everyone knows where to be during your wedding day, as well as what is expected of them.
- Pack a bag for the day—and for the night!
- Get a good night's sleep the night before.
- Charge your phone
- Hope for the best but know that something will go awry.
- Focus on the big picture.
- Enjoy every moment and be present.
- Get married!

CHAPTER TWENTY-THREE

HAPPILY EVER AFTER

Congratulations! You've tied the knot! Now you can relax with your spouse and bask in the newlywed glow. There are still some last tasks to tackle, but the timeline isn't quite so nerve-wracking. You mainly need to tie up loose ends, express thanks, and ensure that you've got a handle on married life. (Read: you're expected to take care of yourself even more now.)

GIFTS

Wedding gifts might continue to arrive after your wedding ceremony. Arrange for someone to pick them up from your doorstep on a daily basis if you're away on your honeymoon. If you are merging households after your wedding, change your mailing address via the US Post Office website to ensure that all your mail is forwarded to your new home and change the delivery address on all of your gift registries.

THANK-YOU NOTES

For your own sanity and reputation, I hope you've kept up with sending thank-you notes upon the receipt of all gifts. I cannot emphasize enough how thoughtful it is to send thank-you notes and how hurt or disappointed gift-givers are when they don't receive a handwritten note of thanks to acknowledge the thought, time, and financial effort they put into your present. In fact, I'm in favor of keeping up this classic tradition throughout your lifetime: send written thanks following any gift you receive, both now and in the future.

But a thank-you note is especially expected with wedding gifts. Update your spreadsheet as you send the notes so you can check off who has been thanked for what. Couples should tackle this task together (divide and conquer!). If you haven't already given presents to the people who helped you pay for your wedding, deliver them after the wedding. Some couples wait until the wedding photos are available so they can present a full album or bound book to their loved ones who contributed to the cost of the wedding. Honeymoon souvenirs also make for treasured presents. (However, invest in having them shipped from your honeymoon locale to avoid breakage in your luggage.)

CONTRACTUAL OBLIGATIONS

Though almost all vendors require that their final payments be made before the wedding, you may have arranged with some to make the last payments afterward. Settle up now with any remaining vendors. And if anything went terribly wrong in your wedding that wasn't a natural disaster, don't be afraid to request a partial or full refund from the venue or vendor. Weddings are expensive, and you've paid for a service and a high caliber of professionalism. If you are certain that you didn't receive what you paid for, you're well within your rights to pursue a refund—or even legal action. Did you notice that, at every possible chance throughout the book, I mentioned you should always get the final contract with both your signature and the vendor's? This is what you'll need if you're pursuing any legal action against a vendor or venue.

WEDDING ATTIRE

After all the effort you put into obtaining your wedding ensembles, it's important to treat these clothes with care, whether you're having them cleaned for preservation or returning them to a lender. To avoid stains and wrinkles, hang up your outfit as soon as you take it off. Arrange for an attendant or family member to take all items to a professional cleaner soon after the wedding, especially if you spilled anything on them during the wedding. Enzymes from food and drink can discolor certain fabrics over time. If you're delaying or abstaining from a honeymoon, you can take your wedding attire to the cleaner yourself.

Once gowns are cleaned, professional cleaners place them in a sealed container for storage. Refer to the cleaner for their recommendations based on the fabric and the container, but typically a high and dry place is best for storing your outfit.

RENTALS

If you or your attendants have items to return to shops, everyone is responsible for returning their own items in accordance with the contracts they signed. But giving attendants a friendly reminder can't hurt.

BOUQUETS AND BOUTONNIERES

Bouquets and boutonnieres can be preserved in a multitude of ways: under a dust-free dome, displayed out in the open, or stored away in the freezer. Or pluck off a few petals from several flowers and place them between two slats of clean glass to create an art piece from your wedding flowers.

HONEYMOONS

Honeymoons can be taken immediately following the wedding ceremony or within the first year of marriage. A honeymoon is a romantic trip for reveling in your just-married bliss, relaxing and recuperating after the fun-but-exhausting wedding events, and intimately nestling into each other to set the tone for your marriage.

Honeymoons can last as long as you want and can afford—from a weekend getaway to months traveling the globe. Some couples want to fly away and flop on the beach, while others take this time to create an adventure, perhaps exploring the culture of a historically rich locale.

Mixing relaxation and entertainment is often just the right recipe for a honeymoon. Whether you're honeymooning immediately after your wedding or several months out from the big day, you deserve some downtime as well as an adventure. Give some thought to what you both would enjoy on this trip of a lifetime and plan accordingly. Making each other happy is an honorable goal, and if your honeymoon meets both your needs and your partner's, there's a great chance you can accomplish this.

TEN TIPS FOR A FABULOUS HONEYMOON

1. **Set a budget**: Traveling can be expensive, and your honeymoon deserves its own financial planning considerations. Long before your wedding, budget what you can afford to spend on this trip, and set that amount aside in your spreadsheets as an untouchable item. Determining your budget for your honeymoon helps with defraying the costs as well, since the earlier you book your airfare and hotel accommodations, the more money you'll save. Your honeymoon budget should include not only travel and lodging costs but also the cost of meals, travel snacks, souvenirs, sightseeing, tips, and pampering experiences, such as a couple's spa treatment.

2. **Don't leave right away**: It used to be customary for the newlyweds to head to the airport just after their big send-off at the reception, and couples still often plan to fly the morning after their wedding, but there are several reasons to reconsider doing this. First, the sheer exhaustion of getting married can make traveling the next day miserable. Saying "I do" doesn't take much energy, but it's all the work you've done up until that point that makes you so tired. You'll also be worn out by mental fatigue from carrying so much extra information in your mind and worrying about everything getting done—even if you've had a huge team of helpers. And you probably still have loved ones in town for the wedding, and it's a kind gesture to stick around and enjoy them while you can.

3. **Travel safely and with caution**: The world is not yet our oyster. There are thousands of places around the globe with laws forbidding LGBTQ+ people from entering their region and/or giving authorities the right to detain and arrest people suspected of engaging in same-gender sexual relations. Where laws are in place that allow discrimination, local law enforcement as well as residents and tourists are even more likely to harass or hurt you simply for existing, let alone for any public displays of affection. Do your research—on equallywed.com and LGBTQ-specific travel websites as well as through LGBTQ-oriented travel agents and referrals from friends—to find destinations that you'll not only enjoy for their accommodations, food, art, activities, and vistas but also for providing a safe place to honeymoon.

4. **Surprise your new spouse**: How many times have you been on vacation and yearned for just a couple more days? Give your dear one the fabulous gift of extending the honeymoon. Secretly call their boss and extend their time off from work so you can enjoy the honeymoon longer, either away from home by adding a new leg to the trip or after you return. Other surprises could be pre-planned activities or restaurant reservations and special gifts waiting for your spouse in your hotel room, such as chilled Champagne or tickets to a local entertainment event.

5. **Try new things and places**: A culturally rich experience on trips not only engages you with the locals and their way of life but can also enrich your memory vault. Your honeymoon is the trip of all trips—the trip launching your marriage as a copiloted adventure. Experiencing different activities, dishes, and sights together will bring you closer and strengthen your bond no matter how long you've been coupled up.

6. **Try a buddy moon**: Enjoy some time alone together in the early part of your honeymoon and then have friends or another couple or two join you for the end of your trip.

Love Note

The fact that we have marriage equality in the United States of America does not guarantee your safety as a member of the LGBTQ+ community at home or abroad. It's still absolutely necessary that you create living wills and advance health care directives—and keep copies with you at all times, especially when you're traveling. No matter how our world progresses in acceptance, it's still important to hope for the best but prepare for the worst. If either of you is in an accident, gets sick enough to be hospitalized, has surgery, or dies, each of you will want the other to be able to legally remain by your side as your spouse and to make decisions for your care. Your spouse alone knows your wishes more than anyone else, but unfortunately, when LGBTQ+ people become critically ill or die, their partners frequently get pushed out of the way—out of the room and out of the experience—because of homophobia and transphobia. Be armed with all legal papers, your lawyer's phone number, and emergency plans.

7. **Consider the children:** If you have children from a previous relationship, you might consider bringing them along on your honeymoon. This is perfectly acceptable if both of you are in full enthusiastic support of this arrangement. The trip could get strained if only one of you wants to have the children come, and that's a tough way to begin a marriage. This is true even if the children are from your current relationship (though in this case you'll probably more easily come to an agreement that doesn't feel like one of you is being appeased). If you'd like the children to join you for only part of the honeymoon, enlist parents or friends to help them travel safely to and from your honeymoon location.

8. **Leave a trail:** Anytime you're leaving the country, make sure that at least one person knows everything about your whereabouts, including your basic itinerary, names and numbers of the places where you'll be staying, and flight dates and numbers.

9. **Pets, presents, kids, mail, and plants:** Be sure to have a plan for everything and everyone who depends on you to be taken care of in your absence. Wedding presents and mail may pile up outside of your door or in your mailbox, so have a trusted individual do daily pickups. If you're leaving kids behind, make sure to provide their caregiver with your itinerary, instructions for emergencies, plenty of food, pocket money for activities, and special notes for your children reminding them how loved they are. Make sure the person looking after your pets has all the food, keys, and supplies that they'll need and a little extra money in case food runs out.

10. **Indulge:** Whether you're a hedonist or a frugal money minder, pamper yourselves with some luxuries during this once-in-a-lifetime trip. You've probably taken romantic trips together before, and you'll surely have more romantic trips in the future, but this is likely to be your only honeymoon. Live it up with spa treatments, a gourmet meal, tickets to a concert or sporting event, or extravagant adventure activities, such as parasailing or a day trip on a yacht, or a cultural immersion experience, such as a cooking class or a guided tour.

HOME SWEET HOME: AFTER THE HONEYMOON

CHANGING YOUR NAME(S) • Although LGBTQ+ couples change their names less often than heterosexual couples do, many do go this route. If you decide to change your name, see page 189 for a rundown on how to do this legally. There are several reasons why people want to change their name after marriage. Some want to assume one family name or get rid of another married last name; others may wish to adhere to tradition. Perhaps most critically, some LGBTQ+ couples change their names for reasons of safety and health: if you live or travel in hostile environments, sharing the same last name can make it easier to speak for each other legally, visit each other in hospital rooms, make important health decisions for each other, and, if there's a death, bring your partner's body home to be laid to rest.

A modern tradition among some LGBTQ+ couples is to assume an entirely new last name—whether it's a combination of their current last names, another family name, or just a word that is meaningful to them. You can also hyphenate your last names, or select one of your last names that you both will use. The one whose last name will now be shared might take the other one's last name as their new legal middle name.

SELECTING WEDDING PHOTOS • Prior to the wedding, it's standard to have reached an agreement with your photographer about when you can expect to receive your edited wedding images. The photographer will usually provide a website where you can review them and select your favorites for ordering. You may have purchased a specific package or even a CD of all high-resolution, watermark-free images to be mailed to you. If you need to review images from your photographer, do so quickly, before the momentum fades and the hubbub of regular life whisks the idea into the corners of your mind. If you wait too long, your photographer will have moved on to other clients, making it harder to get in touch, request special changes, and, unfortunately, receive the best service.

SUBMITTING YOUR WEDDING FOR PUBLICATION • After you tie the knot, consider submitting your wedding for publication. You can send a wedding announcement to your local newspaper for a formal announcement. Or consider submitting your wedding story and photos to a wedding magazine or blog such as equallywed.com for an editorial feature. Not only is it a feel-good experience for you and your loved ones to be able to share in your joy (and witness all your hard work!), but future couples of all orientations enjoy being able to draw inspiration from your specific personalization, your fashion choices, and the narrative of your love story.

ENJOY AND CHERISH YOUR MARRIAGE

Whether you've been together for one year or twenty, allow the meaning of being married to one another fully take hold of you. It's not just a formality or a piece of paper! You may need to make adjustments in your lives, such as moving in together, establishing boundaries with families, and either committing to monogamy or, if you had an open relationship prior to your wedding, updating your previous agreements or making new ones. This is just the beginning of your everlasting devotion to one another. You've made the ultimate commitment to your partner to honor and cherish them. No matter what comes your way, you'll be facing it together—officially.

Tasks to Tackle

- ▨ Return or preserve your wedding attire.
- ▨ Write thank-you notes to everyone who should get one.
- ▨ Enjoy a romantic trip with your new spouse.
- ▨ Get your wedding photos back.
- ▨ Submit your wedding to a newspaper, magazine, or blog.
- ▨ Update all concerned parties about any name changes.
- ▨ Celebrate your marriage!

WEDDING PLANNING CHECKLIST

TWELVE-PLUS MONTHS BEFORE

☐ Scout reception sites in your area until you find the perfect venue.

☐ Start your guest list! Decide approximately how many people you want to invite. Before compiling your list, request wish lists from both sets of parents (or whoever is helping you foot the bill).

☐ Having an engagement party? Set a date, draft a guest list, and order the invitations. Remember: don't invite anyone who won't be invited to the wedding.

☐ Book your reception site. This determines everything else about your wedding: decor, formality, and sometimes even the date.

TWELVE MONTHS BEFORE

☐ Congrats on your engagement! It's time to get the word out via something creative—perhaps a surprise engagement party or even just through social media.

☐ Gather your thoughts and ideas in one place like a notebook, folder, or binder.

- [ ] Imagine the style you want for your wedding.

- [ ] Choose your wedding colors.

- [ ] Decide on a wedding budget and figure out who's making financial contributions to the wedding.

- [ ] Protect your engagement rings. Make sure you have them appraised and insured.

- [ ] Consider what kind of ceremony you want to have and what kind of officiant would be best to preside over it. Religious? Civil? Spiritual?

- [ ] Choose a wedding date and time, and finalize these details after getting clearance from important guests (parents, siblings, and grandparents), from the ceremony and/or reception locations, and from the ceremony officiant.

- [ ] Interview caterers. Find an equality-minded caterer in equallywed.com's vendor directory.

- [ ] Find a ceremony site if it will be different from your reception site.

- [ ] Hire your caterer and plan out your menu with a good understanding of cost per person.

- [ ] Start shopping for wedding attire. (Dresses can take six months to be made.)

- [ ] Finalize your wedding guest list. When you're done, enter everything into your organization system.

- [ ] Try on wedding attire, and consider doing so without your partner, even if you're wearing matching attire. There's something extraordinary about waiting until the wedding day for the big reveal. Find an equality-minded store in equallywed.com's vendor directory so that no one rains on your parade.

- [ ] Research photographers and videographers in your area. If this is an important part of your day, hire these professionals twelve months in advance to ensure their availability for your day.

ELEVEN MONTHS BEFORE

- [ ] Start your gift registry.

NINE MONTHS BEFORE

- [ ] Look for and start interviewing ceremony officiant candidates.
- [ ] Interview wedding coordinators or planners. Find equality-minded planners on equallywed.com.
- [ ] Start thinking about what you and your partner might like to wear to your wedding.
- [ ] Hire a wedding coordinator (if you're having one) and sign the wedding coordinator contract.
- [ ] Choose your wedding party, including honor attendants, a ring bearer, and a flower child. Also consider giving a part (ceremony reader, guest-book attendant, candle lighter) to important friends and family members outside of the wedding party.
- [ ] Make a list of family wedding customs or cultural traditions you might want to incorporate into your ceremony or reception.
- [ ] Sign the catering contract and send in a deposit.
- [ ] Research lighting and any other audio or visual equipment you might want to rent.
- [ ] Set up appointments with wedding florists to discuss options for flowers or greenery.
- [ ] Figure out invitations and stationery.
- [ ] Hire your photographer and videographer. Decide on the packages you want, sign the contracts, and send in your deposits.
- [ ] Narrow down your attire options, make a final decision, and then buy/order your outfits.
- [ ] Decide on a florist and send in a deposit to reserve their services.
- [ ] Have engagement photos taken. (These are great to use on your save-the-date announcements and wedding website.)

- [ ] Think about your attendants' outfits and what you want them to look like and what might look best on them.
- [ ] Search for local cake bakers to make your wedding cake. Your caterer is a great source for leads.
- [ ] Think about surprising your partner with a groom's or broom's cake.
- [ ] Book your honeymoon. Check out equallywed.com for equality-minded destinations that are safer for LGBTQ+ travel.
- [ ] If you don't already have them, make sure you and your partner have up-to-date passports.
- [ ] Think about wedding hairstyles you like, and start researching hairstylists and makeup artists in your area.

EIGHT MONTHS BEFORE

- [ ] Research reception bands or DJs. Make time to meet them and hear their work.
- [ ] Create a wedding website.
- [ ] Update your organizational system to enter gifts you've received thus far and note whether you've sent thank-you notes.

SIX MONTHS BEFORE

- [ ] Start or increase a body-positive regime of moving your body more and making smart food choices.
- [ ] Book your reception band or DJ, sign the reception music contract, and make a deposit.
- [ ] Find ceremony musicians in your area and listen to demos. Also start forming an idea of what style of ceremony music or specific songs you want.
- [ ] Finalize wedding party attire selections. Narrow down the options and let your attendants know which one you've chosen so

that they can schedule their fittings. If you have an honor attendant, they can relay this information to the other attendants.

☐ Prepare for out-of-town guests and set aside a block of rooms at nearby hotels.

☐ Complete your registry. Select three times as many items as you have guests, with a wide range of price points.

☐ Order save-the-dates and send them out to all your guests.

☐ Book your cake baker, choose a wedding cake design, and send in a deposit once you've signed the wedding cake contract.

☐ Make sure out-of-town attendants have ordered their attire or that you have collected the necessary measurements from them. Then ask everyone to order their attire and confirm with you or your honor attendant when they do.

☐ Finalize the ceremony music contract with your musicians and pay your deposit.

☐ Finalize your invitation wording.

☐ Finalize the menu and service details with the caterer.

☐ Research wedding insurance (if necessary) and purchase it at this time.

☐ Work on invitation wording and figure out the design you want.

☐ Order your wedding invitations and/or wedding announcements.

☐ Browse centerpiece photos and figure out what you like, be it flowers, plants, candles, or other creative ideas. If it's flowers you want, make sure the ones you like are in season on your wedding day.

☐ Go over the proposal with your florist. Decide on your floral style, choose your wedding flowers, and settle on a final price. Once you're certain the contract outlines everything you agreed upon, sign it.

☐ Book a calligrapher in your area (if you're using one).

☐ Figure out everything you need to rent that your caterer and venue aren't providing (linens, tables, chairs, tent, outdoor bathrooms, etc.).

FIVE MONTHS BEFORE

☐ Select songs for the first dance and other special moments in your reception.

☐ Plan the rehearsal dinner. Look for rehearsal dinner sites in your area and provide the host (sometimes the parents) with contact information for your attendants and any other guests.

FOUR TO SIX MONTHS BEFORE

☐ Address your invitations or give them to your calligrapher with your address spreadsheet.

☐ Select accessories (shoes, jewelry, cuff links) for your attendants. You can buy these items or let them know how to purchase them.

☐ Choose a marriage contract (a ketubah or any other contract required by your religion) for the ceremony, especially if you live outside of the United States in a region that doesn't legally recognize your marriage.

☐ Start a beauty and grooming regimen and make appointments at a nearby spa (facials, massages) or dentist (professional teeth whitening).

☐ Buy wedding bands. If one or both of you have engagement rings, select something complementary.

☐ Buy, rent, or make the ceremony decor and reception decorations that aren't provided by your florist or venue (chuppah, aisle runner, program basket, etc.).

☐ Decide on wedding favors.

☐ Double-check that your attendants have bought their attire and accessories.

- ☐ Having a wedding shower? A couple's shower? A bach party? Talk to your honor attendants about any pre-wedding party plans.
- ☐ Having one or more showers? Make sure your hosts know who you want invited.

FOUR MONTHS BEFORE

- ☐ Plan out the ceremony with your beloved and your officiant.
- ☐ Book a wedding-night hotel room.
- ☐ Book the rehearsal dinner site and finalize menu plans.
- ☐ Make sure your out-of-town guests know all the details about available hotels and any room blocks you've set up. A great place to do this is through your wedding website and/or your wedding app.
- ☐ Finalize all honeymoon travel reservations, including flights and rooms.
- ☐ Sign up for professional dance lessons at a dance studio near you or start choreographing your first dance.
- ☐ Pick up your invites (or finish working on them) so you can get ready to send them out.
- ☐ Go to your post office or the USPS website and browse specialty stamps you might want to use on your invitations.
- ☐ If you're taking an international honeymoon, find out what vaccinations you need before entering the country.

THREE TO FOUR MONTHS BEFORE

- ☐ Get any special lingerie, binders, shapewear, or underwear in time for your first wedding dress or suit fitting, especially if they'll be made with thin, sheer, or white fabrics.
- ☐ Finalize the ceremony song list. Tip: make sure whoever is providing your ceremony music knows which version of the songs you're thinking of, especially instrumentals.

- [ ] Confirm your attendants' attire delivery date (if you are handling the order).
- [ ] Research which insurance policies (health, auto, homeowner's, life) you and your partner can combine.

TWO TO FOUR MONTHS BEFORE

- [ ] Send out invitations at least eight weeks before the wedding. Be sure to add extra postage for overseas guests.
- [ ] Envision the ceremony programs. Decide what you want included and whether to hire someone to design them.
- [ ] Finalize ceremony readings and reach out to the people you want to read at your ceremony.
- [ ] Schedule your outfit attire fittings and confirm delivery dates.
- [ ] If your caterer isn't providing alcohol for your reception, now is the time to purchase the liquor, wine, Champagne, and mixers.

TWO MONTHS BEFORE

- [ ] Plan day-of transportation for yourselves, your wedding party, and your guests (as needed).
- [ ] Plan out your ceremony vows, especially if you're writing your own.
- [ ] Figure out where everyone will park for the reception and whether you need to create signs or directions for guests.
- [ ] Having children at your wedding reception? Plan for a kids' activity table and/or a babysitter.
- [ ] Confirm out-of-town guest hotel reservations. Check with the hotel to make sure that you don't need to block out more rooms.
- [ ] Live in a region that legally recognizes your marriage? Research local marriage license requirements.
- [ ] Have your first attire fitting (bring all undergarments and shoes).

- [ ] Buy gifts for your wedding party, including your honor attendants, attendants, flower child, ring bearer, and ushers.

- [ ] Decide on a guest book or other place for guests to sign in and leave you their well wishes.

- [ ] Figure out your "something old, something new, something borrowed, and something blue" if you want to include that custom in your wedding.

FOUR TO SIX WEEKS BEFORE

- [ ] Work on escort cards. Buy materials (if you're making your own) or work out the design with your stationer (if you're having them done). Also, make sure you give typed names to the calligrapher if you're using one.

ONE MONTH BEFORE

- [ ] Have your final attire fitting.

- [ ] Write thank-you notes for any gifts you received at the showers, if you haven't already.

- [ ] Finish up your ceremony programs.

- [ ] Have hair (and makeup) trial runs and finalize your wedding day beauty and grooming appointments. If you're wearing a veil or other hairpiece, bring it to make sure it works with your style.

- [ ] Send out rehearsal dinner invitations, via email or phone if it'll be casual.

- [ ] Wrap all gifts for the wedding party and write each attendant a nice note.

- [ ] Get the marriage license, if you're able, and make appointments for blood tests (if necessary). Check when the license expires.

- [ ] If your home region doesn't recognize your marriage, consider drawing up your own marriage certificate for your officiant, you and your partner, and your honor attendants to sign.

- ☐ Confirm wedding night and honeymoon reservations.

- ☐ Finalize your ceremony. Schedule a follow-up meeting (by phone or in person) with the officiant to go over ceremony timing and details.

- ☐ Confirm with your insurance company that your rings and gifts are covered.

- ☐ Make sure your DJ/band knows which songs you definitely want played and which songs you definitely don't want them to play.

- ☐ Finalize and purchase all your accessories: jewelry, clutch, bow tie, cuff links, collar stays, shoes.

- ☐ Plan out where everyone will sit at the reception with a seating chart, and determine how you'll let people know where to sit, such as place cards and an escort table or wall.

TWO TO FOUR WEEKS BEFORE

- ☐ Pick up your wedding attire.

- ☐ If you are changing your name, research the process in your county. If your state doesn't recognize your marriage, changing your name is far more difficult and time-consuming. It's fine to wait until after the wedding. But if your state does acknowledge your marriage, then the paperwork is the same as it is for heterosexual couples.

- ☐ Work out a day-of schedule to time out all the details, from where you'll get ready to how you and your partner are getting there, to where everyone else will get dressed, to when vendors can arrive to set up. Make sure someone you trust besides your partner has a copy of this schedule.

- ☐ Finalize (in writing) any special ceremony details like readings or other traditions with your officiant.

- ☐ Call your reception site manager and make sure your vendors all have access to the site when they need it.

- ☐ Call guests who haven't RSVP'd for the wedding and rehearsal dinner.

- [ ] Plan separate or combined parties (cocktails, a restaurant lunch, or maybe lunch at your place) where you and your partner can thank your attendants for all their help.

- [ ] Shop and pack for the honeymoon.

- [ ] Compile a "must-take" photo list for your photographer. Also reconfirm location, date, and time with your photographer. If you haven't already, ask what their backup plan is if they get sick.

ONE TO TWO WEEKS BEFORE

- [ ] Write letters to each other to exchange on your wedding night.

- [ ] Make sure everyone who has a role at your wedding—from managing the guest book to ushering to handing out boutonnieres or bouquets—knows what you want them to do and when to do it.

- [ ] If you're having a receiving line, determine the order in which you want everyone to stand.

- [ ] Give the caterer the final head count. Confirm all catering setup instructions and menu items. If you're having buffet tables, make sure the caterer knows about any decor the florist is providing for them.

- [ ] Make sure your transportation providers have a schedule and addresses for pickups on your wedding day.

- [ ] Prepare your wedding toasts or thanks to friends and family. If you want a certain family member or friend to make a toast, consider mentioning it to them now. Not everyone's up on the etiquette like you are.

- [ ] Make sure you and your partner have each tried on your entire wedding outfits before the wedding day to ensure that it all still fits.

- [ ] Confirm all final payment amounts with your vendors.

- [ ] Confirm delivery locations, times, and final arrangement count with your florist.

- [ ] Confirm location, date, and time with your videographer.
- [ ] Give the seating chart to the caterer, the reception site manager, or the host.
- [ ] Designate who (reception site manager, coordinator, close friend) will meet, greet, and handle each vendor on your wedding day.
- [ ] Confirm date, location, time, and playlist with the band/DJ and with ceremony or cocktail hour musicians.
- [ ] In planning some private time together after the ceremony to bask in the freshly married bliss, remember to invite your photographer if you want that moment captured.
- [ ] Finalize all the details with your wedding party about the rehearsal and the ceremony itself (dates, times, directions, duties).
- [ ] Distribute wedding-day directions, schedules, and contact lists to all parents (or other significant people), attendants, and vendors.
- [ ] Make sure your wedding website (and app, if applicable) is up to date with any last-minute changes.
- [ ] Put together an overnight bag for your wedding night (toiletry essentials, love letters for one another, sexy lingerie, JUST MARRIED T-shirts) and designate someone to deliver it to the hotel for you.
- [ ] Confirm toasts with people, such as your honor attendants. If you want your DJ to open the floor up to guests, make sure the DJ knows that.

ONE WEEK BEFORE

- [ ] Get your final haircuts.
- [ ] Get manicures and pedicures (no matter how you identify, everyone can benefit from some buffing and cuticle trimming) and confirm your wedding day beauty and grooming appointments.

- ☐ Leave a copy of your honeymoon itinerary with someone in case of emergency.

- ☐ Plan for any wedding gifts (and cash) brought to the ceremony or reception by designating someone to take care of them at the end of the night.

- ☐ Put final payments and cash tips for vendors in marked envelopes and give them to a designated family member or friend to distribute on your wedding day.

- ☐ Organize a last-minute emergency kit (pain reliever, makeup, safety pins, mints, deodorant remover, etc.). Also make sure you have everything together for your outfit.

- ☐ Arrange for someone to go by your house while you're on your honeymoon to pick up the mail (especially late wedding gifts).

ONE TO THREE DAYS BEFORE

- ☐ Confirm all honeymoon travel plans (including transportation to the airport).

- ☐ If you're heading straight for your honeymoon the day after your wedding, arrange for a close friend or family member to pick up your wedding attire and other personal belongings at the hotel after you depart.

- ☐ Arrange for someone to bring home your cake, gifts, flowers, leftover favors, monogrammed napkins, etc. If you've decided to freeze the top layer of your wedding cake (to be eaten at your first anniversary) and to preserve your bouquets or boutonnieres, be sure this person knows how to do those things.

ONE DAY BEFORE

- ☐ Rehearse the ceremony with your officiant and wedding party.

- ☐ Enjoy your rehearsal dinner, but don't drink too much.

- ☐ Hand off the guest book and pens to a trusted friend to bring to the reception site.
- ☐ If your wedding is in the morning, set your alarm and arrange for a backup.
- ☐ Get a full night's rest.

WITHIN ONE MONTH

- ☐ If you didn't give them out at the rehearsal dinner, mail gifts to your parents or other important people to thank them for their help and support.
- ☐ Make sure all vendor bills have been paid in full.
- ☐ Update the Social Security Administration, your employer, the department of motor vehicles, your bank, and other accounts about your name change.
- ☐ Once your name has been changed legally, update your wills.
- ☐ If you haven't already, meet with an attorney to draw up advanced health care directives with your new legal names so that you'll be able to make important decisions for each other. Unfortunately, being legally married doesn't always protect you from being discriminated against as an LGBTQ+ couple, either domestically or abroad.
- ☐ While you wait for your photographer's proofs to come in, ask your friends to send you their photos from your wedding and organize them in an online album. Make sure to send a few to *Equally Wed* (editors@equallywed.com) for editorial consideration for a Real Wedding article!
- ☐ If you used a videographer, find out when you can expect your edited wedding video.

WITHIN TWO MONTHS

- ☐ Write and send thank-you notes.

RESOURCES

The following list contains sources I consulted in writing this book. Please note that several of these sources are websites that were active at the time of this writing. Websites do change or expire on the Internet, so some of those listed below may no longer be active at the time you are reading this book.

BOOKS

- Anna Post and Lizzie Post, *Emily Post's Wedding Etiquette* (Harper-Collins Publishers, 2014).
- Mindy Weiss with Lisbeth Levine, *The Wedding Book: The Big Book for Your Big Day* (Workman Publishing Company, Inc., 2007).

WEBSITES

- Equally Wed, equallywed.com
- GLAAD, glaad.org
- Blue Nile, bluenile.com
- The Knot, theknot.com

ACKNOWLEDGMENTS

Because books for and by the LGBTQ+ community are generally limited in availability, I am overflowing with gratitude that *Equally Wed* was given an opportunity to be traditionally published and made available to a loving community. This book wouldn't have been possible without the business savvy, cheerleading, and all-around booming support from my agent, Maura Teitelbaum, who strongly believed not only that this book deserved to be on the shelves alongside other major wedding books, but also that there was a market for it. We just needed to find the right publisher who believed in *Equally Wed* as much as we did. And we found our champion with Seal Press, a wonderful and diverse publishing house that I'm proud to be a part of. My eternal thanks go to Stephanie Knapp, my inexhaustible and cheerful editor, for considering me in the first place, and then trusting the message I wanted to convey here in these pages. To my copyeditor, Cynthia Buck, and my project editor, Amber Morris, your valuable work on this book is incredibly appreciated.

The ultimate utterings of appreciation are for my wife, Maria, who never doubted that this book needed to exist, who believed that I was the only person who could write it, who managed on her own our insanely energetic young twin boys while I finished the final chapters, who still makes me weak in the knees, and who gave me the best wedding present imaginable: her unwavering and eternal love.

To my sons, Leonardo and Rocco, it is the highest honor and my greatest achievement to be one of your mothers. I hope that when you grow up, everyone's weddings and marriages are treated with respect—and are legally recognized everywhere.

To the spirit of my father and my brother in the great beyond: I feel your love and encouragement daily.

Clare Connell, thank you for providing the perfect writer's retreat in the woods and for always believing in me. Colleen Oakley, your encouragement as one of my dearest friends and insight as a fellow writer is unparalleled and most appreciated. Anne Chertoff, your wedding wisdom throughout the years has broadened my own knowledge, and I am indebted to your generosity of time and friendship. Ron Ben-Israel, thank you for lending your support and contributions to *Equally Wed* and equallywed.com, and for (almost!) never questioning all my crazy ideas. Liz Gudmundsson, thank you for sharing your flower knowledge with me and for inspiring me with your sweet and creative spirit. Bethel Nathan, having a welcoming equality-minded officiant to go to with all my ceremonial questions is invaluable. Thank you for your contributions to *Equally Wed*. Shana Perry and Brittney Love, thank you for always being willing to answer my seemingly endless photography-related queries with cheer and candor, and for contributing to *Equally Wed*. Mary Going, thank you for offering your fashion and self-awareness wisdom to my readers. Amber Harrison, thank you for sharing some of your vast knowledge with *Equally Wed* readers. Van Barnes, you put things in perfect perspective for me. One of my deepest wishes is that every reader of this guide will feel well represented, and your advice truly helped to shape that possibility into a reality. Beth Bernstein, thank you for educating me about Jewish weddings and for supporting my dreams while sweetly understanding my quirks. JoAnn Ferraro Gregoli, thank you for candidly answering my questions about how wedding planners operate and how to be a rock-star working mother. To Angela and Rita Burns, and to Jen Colletta, thank you for opening yourself up to a steady stream of questions about your experiences. Alexis Soterakis, your legal and branding acumen is much appreciated. Lesléa Newman, I am so grateful that you allowed me to include your poem, "Break the Glass," in this book. Your work inspires so many, and it's an honor to share this space with you. Lance Bass and Michael Turchin, thank you for wanting to be part of this book, for believing that it needed to be available, and for being outspoken ambassadors for love and equality. To the wedding writers I admire who've inspired me and educated me over the years with your own books—Meg Keene, Mindy Weiss, Emily Post, Anna Post, and Abby Larson—thank you.

To all the couples and wedding professionals who have shared their stories and experiences with me for this book and during the life of *Equally Wed,* your wisdom has helped shape my view of what is possible (anything), what needs to change in the wedding industry (it's ever-evolving), and just how wonderful weddings can be when everyone feels valued and validated.

INDEX

© OUR LABOR OF LOVE

ABOUT THE AUTHOR

Kirsten Palladino is an award-winning writer and editor, and one of the world's most notable experts on LGBTQ+ weddings. She's the cofounder and editorial director of the world's leading online modern LGBTQ+ wedding magazine, *Equally Wed*, and has been featured in many luminary publications and media outlets, from the *New York Times*, *Los Angeles Times*, *Chicago Tribune*, *Lucky* magazine, *The Knot*, and *Time* magazine to ABC News, CNN, NPR, DailyCandy, Politico, and *Glamour* magazine. Her established career in magazines and newspapers made the creation of *Equally Wed* with her wife, Maria, a graphic designer and web developer, an obvious foray into media entrepreneurship when, in planning their own June 2009 nuptials, they encountered cruel exclusion from traditional wedding media outlets and discrimination from wedding professionals. The legally married creative duo launched *Equally Wed* in March 2010. Palladino is an Athens, Georgia, native and an equality activist in both her current city of Atlanta and abroad. In 2016, she founded the Wedding Equality Alliance, an international group of wedding professionals committed to tearing down exclusionary walls in the typically heteronormative wedding industry. Palladino regularly speaks about LGBTQ+ inclusion in the wedding industry and writes about LGBTQ+ weddings and equality on equallywed.com. Learn more about the author at kirsten palladino.com and about *Equally Wed* at equallywed.com.